# Without Explanation

# Without Explanation

*A True Story of Love and Loss in the Jungle*

ROD JASMER

Archean
MEDIA PRODUCTIONS

Archean Media Productions, LLC,
P.O. Box 827, Park City, UT 84060
Archean-Media.com

Editors: C. S. Lakin, Kristen Corrects, Kim Foster, Blue Otter, and Eve Gumpel

Printed in the United States
FIRST EDITION

| | |
|---|---|
| Names: | Jasmer, Rodney M., author. |
| Title: | Without explanation : a true story of love and loss in the jungle / Rod Jasmer. |
| Description: | First edition. \| Park City, UT : Archean Media Productions, [2017] |
| Identifiers: | ISBN: 978-0-9981482-0-5 (paperback) \| 978-0-9981482-1-2 (hardcover) \| 978-0-9981482-2-9 (ebook) \| 978-0-9981482-3-6 (epub) \| LCCN: 2016916116 |
| Subjects: | LCSH: Jasmer, Valerie Jo'an, 1964-2004. \| Jasmer, Rodney M. \| Guatemala--Description and travel--Personal narratives. \| Medical emergencies--Guatemala--Personal narratives. \| Emergency medical services--Guatemala. \| Married people. \| Wives--Death--Personal narratives. \| Bereavement--Personal narratives. \| Widowers--Psychological aspects. \| BISAC: BIOGRAPHY & AUTOBIOGRAPHY / Personal Memoirs. \| FAMILY & RELATIONSHIPS / Death, Grief, Bereavement. \| FAMILY & RELATIONSHIPS / Love & Romance. |
| Classification: | LCC: HQ1058 .J37 2017 \| DDC: 306.88/2--dc23 |

2  4  6  8  10  9  7  5  3  1

# Dedication

This book is dedicated to my children, who, on a daily basis, learn how to face life's dreams and fears without their mother's enduring presence. Try as I might to provide hope and happiness in their lives, I am not, nor can I ever become, their wonderful mother. I can, however, provide continual reminders and insight into her life and the lives she inspired, instilling in them that her physical, mental, spiritual and emotional essence will always reside within them.

# Disclaimer

This book is a memoir. It reflects primarily a two-week period of my life between Wednesday, April 14, 2004, and Tuesday, April 27, 2004. The events, places and people are real. It captures specific scenes as they occurred and provides a representation of actual dialogue through paraphrases of conversations and events.

Besides my own memory of the experience, notes, letters, articles and journals supplement the book. Many detailed interviews took place, some conducted multiple times over a ten-year period. They aided in capturing other individuals' distinct perspectives and firsthand accounts of particular settings. Through these personal interviews, I was able to connect the multitude of activities that happened simultaneously.

I requested permission to use given names for a number of individuals. For all other names and entities referenced in the narrative, particularly those mentioned briefly or residing in other countries, I substituted alternative names.

# Contents

## PART IV – A Long Way to the Unknown

## PART V – A Solemn Return

## PART VI – Simple Words

# Preface

This event changed my life and the lives of many others. From the very beginning of the incident, people wanted to know and understand what happened. What caused this? Where were you? Who helped? How did you get through it? Some people were searching for specific answers or logistical facts; others looked for closure and resolution. I had all these questions and more. However, I simply—and as time grew, desperately—just wanted to put the pieces of an otherwise wonderful life back together.

I knew on the plane ride home from Guatemala that I would someday document these events, though, at the time, I wasn't sure why. I began jotting down notes and random thoughts as they filled my mind. Adjusting to a new and unfamiliar life took much of my time, and I couldn't turn my notes into coherent sentences until early 2008. When I did begin to write, my fingers had little chance of moving fast enough to record the stream of thoughts passing through them to the computer screen. Other times, I found myself transported back to a relic of time, vividly reliving suppressed memories. Some were gloriously magnificent, as we shared so many wonderful times; others were painful.

Raising three young children is demanding and has its own set of time constraints. Within a few months, I found it difficult to focus on both writing and caring for my kids in the way I wanted to. At least, for me, these two passions could not coexist. Now, here I am, more than ten years after Valerie's death, and I am finishing the story that began so long ago.

Over time, the necessity of writing this book has become clearer to me. I want friends and family members to hear the complete story; however, my primary motivation centers on my children. They deserve to know everything regarding their mother's final days and the tragic incident that took her life. Though this event isn't something anyone will likely forget, memories fade, and I am glad I wrote notes about so much of this early on. This memoir is yet another way to honor their mother.

Writing this book has been cathartic for me as well. As I continue to address personal feelings about the events and the great loss of life I have felt over the years, I have placed myself back into each situation, crying often, assuming the burdens once again. Writing was, and continues to be, good therapy. Perhaps others will find solace and strength through the description of this ordeal. The very fact that you are reading this reassures me that memories of Valerie will endure.

My intent was to document events, not necessarily portray my relationship with Valerie, thought several early readers have commented that this book is really a love story. Though far too short, I was fortunate to have had Valerie in my life. Not everyone has the opportunity to share this type of love, and I feel lucky and grateful for the time we spent together. It is precisely this fact that assures me I will once again find true love in my life. I certainly know Valerie would believe so.

Someone else might have reacted much differently than I did when faced with a similar situation. Some may wonder why I completed a certain activity or be surprised that I thought a particular way. In retrospect, I have often wondered about my own behaviors and feelings at the time. I have made peace with each of these and understand they cannot be categorized as either right or wrong, just reactions within the context of an extraordinary circumstance.

Everyone remembers a situation differently. This book captures my remembrances and feelings of the experience as well as those gathered from others who were part of the events. I have not sensationalized or inadvertently omitted any information; I have only tried to describe moments as they dramatically unfolded.

Rod Jasmer

# PART I

*Enthusiasm and Expectations*

# Chapter 1

*Premonition*

---

"I don't think we should go," Valerie said, half shouting the words as she sat up in bed just before midnight. "What if something happens?"

"What? . . . What are you saying? Are you talking about the trip?" I said, rolling toward her.

We hadn't been in bed for very long, so I knew this wasn't part of some unconscious dream. Just as I was about to make light of the situation, I caught a glimpse of her face softly illuminated by the yard light between our house and shed. Valerie was serious. This wasn't the time, if I knew what was best for me, to joke or make light of her fears, no matter how absurd they seemed.

"How can you even think that? What do you think will happen anyway?" I asked.

"I don't know—just what if something does? What if our bus has an accident, and the two of us are killed?"

"Yeah, I understand, Val, but the same thing can happen here," I said, trying to reassure her.

Valerie stared at the blank wall next to the bed with a detached expression. She gave no immediate response, and by the look on her face I knew this was not just a passing thought.

She turned toward me, looking directly into my eyes, and pressed on. "But it would be different there. It just wouldn't be the same—and what about the kids?"

Valerie was right, of course. It would not be the same as being here. That was the point she was trying to make. However, in the middle of the night, after spending the day preparing to depart—the alarm clock only a few hours from blaring—her worries were difficult for me to comprehend.

"Val, we can't predict what will happen," I said. "You're the one who wanted to go on this trip, and now, the night before, you're having second thoughts. Let's get some sleep. We're meeting Jenn and Jeff in just a few hours."

I wasn't sure if my words reassured her or if she was merely tired as well, but she lay back down. "I know, I know. You're right. Let's get some sleep."

For the second time, I closed my eyes, Valerie's words lingering in my mind. I wondered why she would raise such vivid concerns the night before our trip. Within seconds, the conversation drifted from my consciousness.

# Chapter 2

*Past Experience versus Present-Day Existence*

---

Jennifer, Jeff and I worked together in the early days of our careers in the mid-nineties. The small environmental consulting firm in Saint Paul, Minnesota, wasn't without its drama, but, on the whole, it was a stimulating place to work. Jeff and I were both geologists, so we easily related to each other. Jeff had a matter-of-fact personality and a dry sense of humor, and was typically more a man of action than of words—something I could relate to. But his personality was a stark contrast to those of Valerie and Jennifer. Jennifer, whose friends frequently called her Jenn, was vivacious and extroverted, similar to Valerie. Jenn worked in the business side of the company, and after a few years, she and Jeff fell in love and married. Our careers moved in different directions over the years, but our friendship remained.

Our jointly planned trip had been in the making for a long time, but it was during a mid-January dinner at Jenn and Jeff's house that the idea was jump-started.

"We really should go on that trip together soon," Valerie said on that cold evening.

Val's declaration spun us on a number of lively tangents, landing on a week of adventure somewhere near the equator.

The next day we woke not feeling nearly as blissful as we were the night before. As three cute but nevertheless demanding children burst into our room, begging to play, needing something or other and insisting on breakfast, the exotic travel adventure we'd envisioned the night before vanished quickly with the reality of life.

Val and I had some experience traveling, but we were far from experts. In late 1987, we married and made an immediate decision to forgo accepting job offers and climbing the proverbial corporate ladder. Instead, we withdrew all the money we'd saved, packed a few bags—which we managed to fit most of our belongings in—and moved to Australia.

Valerie was the first to secure employment Down Under. She was a dental hygienist, and while the Australian Board of Dentistry allowed only minor duties for dental hygienists, she worked in what some called the hygienist underground. Several of the more progressive dentists in Melbourne recognized the value of an expanded role for the hygienist. Valerie and the dentists would have been in some trouble if they'd been discovered.

Within a few weeks of entering the country, I also found a job as a hydrogeologist, and thus our new life's journey began.

Our relationship was almost as new as our surroundings. During our tremendous two-year stint as residents of Australia, we toured some of the backcountry, and it was there that we cemented our enthusiasm for traveling together.

We knew, even being relatively young, that our time together in this faraway land was unique and one we might never duplicate. We recognized early on that spotting a mother koala in the wild eating a eucalyptus leaf while a baby joey clung to her back and feeling the exhilarating presence of hundreds of sulphur-crested cockatoos flocking and screeching above our heads were likely one-time-only moments in life. For Valerie in particular, our time in Australia meant much more than a fun travel experience. The people and their culture, personalities and beliefs were the things that appealed to Val.

Before returning to America, we took advantage of our location and embarked on an extended overland trek through nine countries in Southeast Asia. Trekking soon seemed as natural as anything else we had done previously. The life we later developed in Linwood, Minnesota, just north of Minneapolis/Saint Paul, had routine, schedules and deadlines—all necessary and normal—but those structuring elements had been nonexistent during our trekking life. No specific agenda, no timed stops, no hotel reservations—just one destination after another, sleeping at bus stations and on park benches, exchanging currency as needed. We moved from country to country, content to experience whatever the day brought.

In our current life, our kids and work had become our priorities, and that was just fine. Alisha, our oldest, was thirteen and in seventh grade. She was in her second year of attending a charter middle school fifteen miles from our house. Erica, our middle daughter, was eleven and in fifth grade and attended the local elementary school with our son, Peter, who was eight and in second grade.

Yes, it had indeed been years since we'd trekked through a country, and because we'd had a taste, thoughts of trekking again never completely went away. We were confident in our hopes that someday we would backpack again, and we both knew exactly where our backpacks were stored.

⌒↬⌒

Jeff and Jenn were veteran trekkers as well, and as our joint adventure gained traction, we considered several locations. We'd heard wonderful things about Belize; the diversity of mountain hiking and ocean snorkeling certainly appealed to Val and me. The proximity of Guatemala and the ancient ruins of Tikal made them a great extension to the trip. Since Jeff and Jenn could speak Spanish reasonably well, the combination seemed to fit perfectly. Though our time would be limited, we'd be trekking again.

However, in my opinion, this wasn't the time to take a vacation. The consequences of previous work-related business decisions had my nerves frazzled, and the issues continued to wear on me. I'd purchased, with my business partner, Dan, the small environmental consulting firm we'd worked for during the previous ten years. The ownership transition had not been a smooth one. We'd taken out second mortgages and borrowed more money from the bank than I thought was even possible.

We worked hard to grow the company, but, like many small business owners, we faced numerous hurdles. Our largest client merged with another company, and any future business with them was questionable. Most of our employees we knew on a personal level, many being our best friends, so downsizing and laying anyone off was difficult to even consider.

In an effort to alleviate some of our debt load, and in order to ensure jobs for everyone, we sold the company in 2003. Shortly after the sale, it became clear we wouldn't realize the full value from selling the firm. We needed to earn over time a large portion of the money we'd hoped to receive. Two pending legal cases, neither of which we were direct parties to, required time and money to deal with, and added to the weight on my mind.

As time moved on and we had yet to finalize the trip and purchase tickets, I began to have second thoughts.

"Val, I'm not sure this is the right time to go. I mean, with all my work stuff going on and you being so busy, do you really want to go?" I asked, wondering if she was having similar thoughts. I knew the questions were more for my own contemplation; I needed to rationalize the trip in my own mind.

Val well knew the pressures I'd been going through and, as always, did what she could to support our life together and me personally. During a hastened morning routine in early March, Val made a point of stopping me.

"Rod, I understand this is very difficult for you, but we'll get through this together."

We both knew that we would. I just needed to change my mind-set somehow.

Later in the day, I noticed a card tucked lovingly into the top pocket of my briefcase. Valerie's words reassured me of our joint commitment to get through life's small struggles together:

> *Rod,*
>     *This will be really hard for you, maybe for a long time, but we'll get through it!*
>     *I'm so proud of you!*
>     *I love you, buddy. . . .*
> *Valerie*

I read it several times, and each time I thought of challenges we'd already overcome. We would get through this, together.

Though I continued to push off the final decision regarding the trip, I knew we needed to act soon if we were going to make it happen.

A week or so later, after tucking the children into bed, Val said, "I think it's a good time to take the trip with Jeff and Jenn. If we don't go now, I'm not sure we ever will."

"But what about your job, church . . . Scouts? Do you think we have the time?" I asked.

"Listen to yourself. I can make it work. It's less than two weeks. You need to make it work in *your* mind," Val replied.

"If you, Jeff and Jenn are all excited, I won't stand in the way. I won't be a stick-in-the-mud either; I'll have a good time. It's just that if anyone is thinking maybe we shouldn't go, I'm okay with bagging the plans."

That was my last effort to hold us back. Even as I said the words, my mind had shifted.

"We can make this happen if we want. We should go," Val said. As she headed out of the room, she stopped and gave me a reassuring smile. I shook my head and started to laugh.

We booked the tickets the next day, March 21, 2004. The plan was in motion.

# Chapter 3

## *The Essentials*

---

**M**y parents lived approximately 150 miles northwest of us, and we arranged for them to stay at our house to care for our children during our ten-day absence. We talked with the kids about Mom and Dad's trip, though I'm not sure how well they understood the details.

Val was busy making final arrangements with the two schools, Girl Scouts, spring sports activities, and a myriad of other things, when I took a call from one of her six siblings. Val's sister Eileen lived the closest to us of all Valerie's family, though still roughly five hours away in Madison, Wisconsin. She wanted to know about our trip, and I gave her the basics.

"Nope, we don't have any hotels booked. We're not really sure where we'll be staying yet," I said. "Definitely no transfers.

We plan to take local transport where we can find it—likely localized buses or getting a ride in someone's personal vehicle. You never know, maybe we'll end up riding with chickens and sleeping in a small shack like we've done before."

My words were neither expected nor comforting to Val's sister, and our discussion did not sit particularly well with her. Eileen had just seen Valerie at her house a week ago, and they hadn't discussed the details of what seemed like an unusual vacation to Eileen. For Val and me, our upcoming adventure was a peek into our past life; to Eileen, it was unsettling.

I took almost the entire day to pack, and though Valerie started packing four hours after me, we finished at the same time. The general travel plan included spending the first few days exploring rain forests and hiking around Mayan ruins in northern Guatemala, then making our way east to enjoy water-related sites in Belize. A few items were required to accomplish these tasks, and at the top of my list was our snorkel gear.

"I know we can rent gear there, but remember what a pain that is? Their equipment never fits properly, and it's usually poor quality. With our own gear, if we see a spot we like, we can just go," I said, trying to justify bringing the bulky equipment.

"I understand, but we can't fit all that in. It'll take up one whole travel pack," Val said, eyeing the stack of snorkels, masks and fins piled against the wall.

"Of course they'll fit. All we need are a few shirts and a pair of shorts," I said, showing Val my pile of clothes that was half the size of the snorkel gear.

"One pair of shorts? Yeah, right. Maybe for you," Val said, laughing.

"I'll tell you what—I'll carry the lot in my pack. You can

bring what you want. Then we'll be able to snorkel anywhere we like." As I pulled other items from my pack, I wondered if the equipment would actually fit.

"Okay, I agree. I'll make some room, too," said Val.

That evening, as we tucked each of the children into their beds, we said our good-byes. We'd be out the door before they woke up the next day. Grandma and Grandpa were ready to take the helm.

# Chapter 4

## Disappearing Sounds

---

The radio alarm sounded at 3:30 a.m. and Val and I were up again. Even the excitement of an impending trip loses some luster with only a couple hours of sleep. Val was first in the shower, as usual, so she could have a little more time to get ready, and I could get an extra five minutes of snoozing by letting her shower first.

Alisha and Erica had their own rooms downstairs, though, with some regularity, one of them would ask to sleep upstairs on the living room couch. According to their reasoning, they always slept much better there. Peter was in the bedroom next to ours, so we tried to be as quiet as possible so as not to wake him.

"Hey, what's the temperature going to be again?" Val asked.

"I don't know, but I'd go with hot," I said. "Did we pack both battery packs for the video recorder? I can't find them with all this snorkel stuff in my pack. Why the hell are we packing all that crap anyway?" I said, half mumbling to myself. The chatter of two people getting last-minute items together continued back and forth.

"Keep it down. Let's not wake up Peter," Val said.

"Oops. Sorry. I'm glad we said good-bye to the kids last night. Do you think Peter is doing any better?"

"He's okay. He's just worried about our trip. I'll tell you about it later. I'm going to write a quick note to the kids. I know I'm going to miss them," Val said, moving into the kitchen.

"Hi," came a tiny, high-pitched voice accompanied by a set of shiny eyes just barely peeking over the back of the living room couch.

"Erica, what are you doing up? Sorry we're so loud," Val whispered to our middle daughter as she finished writing her note to the kids on a small yellow sticky pad.

> ALISHA, ERICA, PETER,
>   We love you! Be good for Grandma & Grandpa.
> Listen! Help out w/ chores. We will miss you.
> Love,
> Mom & Dad

Val stuck the note on the kitchen table and went to give Erica one last hug good-bye. "Be good for Grandma and Grandpa. Love you.

"Rod, where are you going? Jeff and Jenn are probably waiting. Let's go," Val said, taking the stairs down to the entryway.

"I'm just getting some water. The car is started and bags are in," I said, passing Val in the opposite direction.

"Bye, Dad," came Erica's voice from the couch.

"Erica? Hi, Sweetie. I love you. See you in a week or so. Be good for Grandma and Grandpa." I touched her head and made for the kitchen.

Not far away, a little eight-year-old boy lay in a darkened room. Eyes wide, ears perked, listening to the faint words entering the space around him. Our alarm clock had awakened him, and he could see a small sliver of light radiating under his closed bedroom door. He knew his mother and I were getting ready to go to some faraway place without him.

Peter was a light sleeper at times and often heard us getting ready in the mornings. This morning was no exception, though he would not share this moment with me until many years later. As Peter listened intently to the muffled sounds, something about being hot and something about water and pictures, he wondered if he should tell us he was up.

The urge to give us one last hug grew stronger; he knew he would not see us for a while. He was no longer sleepy as his heart began to beat wildly, listening to the early-morning activities outside his room. He thought he'd heard his sister's voice. Maybe he should also get up and say good-bye one last time. He needed one more hug, but not wanting to slow us down, he tucked himself back under his dinosaur blanket.

Just as suddenly as the radio and voices had stirred Peter from his deep sleep, the commotion ended. The light emanating from the hallway under his door was no longer there. The noise of the garage door closing was the last sound remaining, and then, as if the depth of the night was suddenly back, there was nothing. Silence filled his room, gripping him completely.

In an instant, his excitement and bravery were gone, sadness and remorse taking their place. Peter suddenly knew he should've followed his initial instincts to get up and hug us both. He had no idea how that moment would torment him almost daily for the next five years.

# Chapter 5

## *Back on the Travel Bicycle*

As the crow flies, our house was less than three miles from Jenn and Jeff's. We'd decided to meet at the end of our road at 4:15 a.m. to drive to the airport. Traffic was light, as one would expect for an early Thursday morning on April 15, 2004. We dropped Jeff's Ford Explorer at his office and continued to the Park-n-Jet ramp near the Minneapolis/Saint Paul International Airport.

"Nice packs," Jeff said with a grin as we hefted our travel packs from our minivan into the back of the airport shuttle.

"Sure are," I said with an air of pride in my voice. Val and I stole a glance at each other, not sure if Jeff was being sarcastic. It had been a while since we'd used our packs. We'd needed to wipe them out and spray them with a healthy dose of disinfectant to get the musty smell out. Next to the sleekness of

Jeff's and Jenn's packs, ours suddenly looked worn and old, more like canvas suitcases than backpacks. Updating our packs had never crossed our minds. They'd survived our five-month stint of overland travel in the eighties and other expeditions; they could survive this trip. My backpack envy was short-lived, as I was certain we couldn't have fit all our snorkel gear into one of their new-styled packs.

We arrived at the airport in plenty of time and easily made it through security. My frequent business travel came with many negatives, but the company I worked for provided an airport lounge membership, enabling us to grab a light breakfast at one of the Northwest Airlines lounges. We decided not to partake of the free alcoholic beverages (though tempting) and opted instead for orange juice. The partially booked flight to Houston allowed me a complimentary first-class upgrade. Neither Jenn nor Jeff had experienced the front seats previously, and I offered my ticket to them. Jenn insisted Jeff should take it, and without much persuasion, Jeff accepted.

We had a short layover in Houston, just long enough for Jenn, Val and me to grab some food. Jeff was still full from his first-class breakfast.

The 11:50 a.m. departure to Belize City was on time, and our arrival was slightly ahead of schedule. With our passports in hand and our luggage passing customs without incident, we were standing outside the Belize airport by 1:30 p.m. The trip, only in its earliest stages, was already fun.

Immediately the Central American warmth moved into my body, replacing the dry, cool Minnesota spring climate. The temperature and humidity were in the upper eighties, and I began to perspire. I could taste the slightly salty air.

Arriving in a foreign land can bring feelings of excitement as well as anxiety—at least that was the case for Val and me. This time was no exception.

"Remind you of anything?" Val asked.

"Sure does. Feels good to be back in this type of climate. I hope we don't make the same mistakes we made before when entering a new country," I replied.

The excitement of a new place, coupled with a lack of local knowledge, had us boarding the wrong bus in Malaysia and getting swindled by a money exchanger in Indonesia—mishaps we'd long ago chalked up to inexperience.

"The first forty-five minutes can only be better," Valerie said as she started to laugh.

Our first task was arranging transportation to the Cayo District of west-central Belize, just north of the Maya Mountains. We engaged a few local drivers crowded near the exit doors of the airport, and though the first two weren't interested in making the trip so far west, we soon negotiated a ride with Eduardo Jr. We knew it was the luck of the draw when it came to drivers, and we drew a nice hand with Ed Jr. He seemed to know how to drive safely and was a talker, which for us as tourists was a good combination. He provided a running description of sights along the way and occasionally detoured in order to show us a place of interest.

As the day passed, we enjoyed new sights and sounds around every corner. By late afternoon, we arrived at the twin towns of Santa Elena and San Ignacio. Ed Jr. suggested a couple of possibilities for spending the night, and we chose to stay in the much smaller town of Santa Elena at a motel that was also mentioned in our guidebook. We stopped at a group of small buildings, and at first glance, it didn't seem like a place to stay. However, as we gathered our packs and entered the grounds, the small, uncrowded inn looked just fine to settle into for the night.

Val and I found our room and dropped our packs on the floor. We were tired. It could've been the remaining adrenaline from the day's activities, finding ourselves in a tropical setting or a complex celestial fate that I couldn't possibly comprehend, but we fell together and made love in the quaint little room. Though the progression of events would be lost in my mind, its significance would never be.

"I'm hungry," I said, getting out of the bed. "I'm going to look for Jenn and Jeff and see if they want to get something to eat." Looking back at Val, I saw her patented smile. Without speaking she shook her head, indicating she wasn't hungry, and continued looking at me without a word.

After freshening up, I opened the door, looked to my left and saw Jenn and Jeff sitting on a wooden picnic table behind the motel.

"Did you get settled in and have a nice nap?" asked Jenn.

"We sure did," I said, smiling.

I joined them at the picnic table for a beer. After Val's nap, the four of us started walking along open and uncongested roads and across a one-lane bridge into San Ignacio for the evening. Many of the buildings were brightly colored, and the narrow curved streets we were now on suggested we had reached an older part of town. Without a specific destination, and not really knowing where we were going, we didn't find a place to eat until the sun was setting. The funky establishment we eventually located had authentic food, and we enjoyed both the meal and the company. We snapped pictures of the various concoctions on our plates—some food appeared to be looking back at us—and all seemed so exotic and memorable. Even the random skinny cat that jumped up on our table during our meal was good for a laugh.

Though San Ignacio was a destination for people venturing into the mountainous areas of Belize, we saw few other tourists around. We questioned those we did meet about transportation to Guatemala and interesting sights in the area. The cave tours seemed particularly intriguing to Jeff, and we thought if we had time on our way back through the area, that would be a nice side adventure.

On our way back to the hotel, we stopped at a small grocery to purchase some bottled water. As we passed the side of the building, we noticed piping coming out of the back wall and several larger plastic bottles scattered around the area. We hoped there was no link between the outside water spigot and our newly purchased water.

We decided to start our next morning's activities at seven, and not even the loud karaoke party outside our window kept us from our waiting beds. This time, sleep only.

# Chapter 6

## A Great Day

The day dawned with noisy chickens sounding their instinctive alarms and a keen awareness that we were indeed in new surroundings. The day's agenda included crossing from Belize into Guatemala and making our way to Tikal. First up was breakfast with Jenn and Jeff under an outdoor canopy. It seemed to take forever before our order was taken and even longer for the food to arrive. I was eager to get moving, to get on with our adventure, to experience the next thing that might come our way.

Though I understood our current setting was much different than we were used to at home, I hadn't yet slowed my pace to match my surroundings. Valerie must have noticed my anxiety, and after my third "When is the food going to be here?" they all noticed my impatience.

"Rod, slow down; live in the moment. This is part of the adventure and why we came here," Valerie reminded me. She was right again. Val, much more than I, understood this quintessential aspect of life and, for the most part, embraced its meaning to the fullest. It turned out to be a wonderful breakfast.

We soon packed our bags and excitedly set out for the town center to arrange transportation to the Guatemalan border. Jeff had told us about several travel blogs that described less-than-well-intentioned drivers in this area, so we needed a little more caution that day. From our meanderings the previous night, we knew the town center was some distance away. We just hoped that, once we arrived, we could find at least one driver willing to take us to the border. Less than a quarter mile from the motel, a late-model Range Rover slowed down alongside us, and a friendly voice asked in well-spoken English if we would like a ride into town.

"No, we're fine, but thank you," Val said.

A little farther down the road, another vehicle slowed down. Its driver waved and pointed his hand to the backseat, motioning for us to get in for a ride.

"No, thanks. *Gracias*," Valerie said with a friendly wave and a smile. No one said anything immediately, but it wasn't long before we realized we'd made a mistake. A combination of early-morning Belize heat, overpacked backpacks, and not knowing exactly where we were going made the offers of motorized transportation grow much more appealing.

"If anyone else stops to give us a ride, let's say yes," I said to my fellow travelers.

"I agree with that," Jeff said with a grin and a slight chuckle.

I turned and winked at Val, who stuck out her tongue at me. It was the beginning of another good day.

Along our path to San Ignacio we were greeted by an expansive, beautiful bridge spanning the Macal River. Crossing over, we noticed several people bathing and doing laundry in the water below. I wondered if this was a daily event or just a Friday ritual. On the other side of the river, the scene of people selling their goods at an open-air market reinvigorated us.

As we neared the spot our travel books suggested would be a likely place to negotiate a ride to the border, we sharpened our wits. We were determined not to become victims of those who might take advantage of unsuspecting foreigners along this stretch of road. The plan was to speak with several people, then decide as a group which driver to select. Undaunted, the four of us approached the area. Before we knew it, Jeff and I had negotiated and secured a driver and vehicle, completely disregarding our self-imposed rules.

"So much for your well-laid-out plan, guys," Val said as she smiled at Jenn.

Both the car and driver did as we'd hoped, and the short trip to the border was pleasant and incident-free. The second leg of the day's journey was complete.

As we exited the vehicle, people immediately surrounded us vying for our attention. They knew our likely destination would require Guatemalan currency and a driver to get us there. Trying not to be rude, we fended them off and gathered our packs from the back of the van.

Our first task was to make our way to the Belize border-control building, a small stucco structure situated roughly twenty-five feet from the road. We handed our passports to the man behind the open sliding-glass window, obtained the required exit stamp, and paid the obligatory departure tax. From there, we moved past a raised pole gate and walked along a small dirt road into Guatemala.

No matter how many times I have crossed a country's border, it's always exhilarating and a little intimidating to do so on foot. There is a sense of security in a vehicle, a feeling of protection you simply do not have when walking from one country to another.

Guatemalan customs was our first stop just over the border to obtain our entry permits. Though the line was not long, we noticed that we were not getting any closer to the windows. Eventually Jeff and I caught on to the locals' game of budging, and we became a little more aggressive in wedging our way to the front of the line.

"You guys are a foot taller than everyone else," Jenn said. "I'm glad you used your size to your advantage," she said, teasing.

With our permission slips to continue our journey in the new country, we exchanged a small amount of US dollars for Guatemalan quetzals and once again hired a local driver. Our driver must have decided the more the merrier, and to our surprise, he solicited two other travelers. Caroline, from France, and Thomas, from Germany, became our riding companions on our way to Tikal. The only way to fit into one of the smallest vans I'd ever seen was to fasten our travel packs to the roof, then carefully maneuver our seven bodies into the vehicle.

The roads we'd traveled the day before and that morning from the town center roundabout in San Ignacio to the border were in relatively good shape. This road was not. I wondered if we were even on the main road or if the driver had taken some off-map back way. The dirty, dusty road was full of curves and endless potholes, making the roughly fifty-mile trip to the park's boundary take much longer than expected.

This driver wasn't the talkative cultural narrator we'd experienced the day before. A nod and a half smile were all we could get out of him. The questions we asked him seemed to make him as nervous as we were with his driving. We eventually stopped asking questions and trusted he would find his way to our destination.

It had been a while since Jenn and Val had spent time together, and they dove headfirst into conversation. Even here, taking in this new and wonderful place, their conversation quickly turned to children. Val described each of our children's lives, how one child was doing this and the other one that. She detailed their personalities, their strengths, how they differed yet were alike in so many ways. She explained how she envisioned her children as teenagers and young adults, describing to Jenn how their traits would likely reflect their character as they grew. Val's descriptions fascinated Jenn, and she would not forget the conversation.

"Peter is a little scared about us going on the trip," Val said. "Jenn, it was so sweet. Peter asked me, 'Who's going to rub my back, Mom?' I had to promise him I would rub his back extra long when I get back home."

"Oh, that's so cute. I'm sure it must be hard on him with you being gone," Jenn said.

"It is. Once I'm back home, I'll make sure to rub his back every night before bedtime," Val declared.

Jenn and Jeff had been trying to have children for some time, and Valerie's descriptions only cemented Jenn's desire to have a child, whether naturally or by adoption. Val encouraged Jenn to continue their efforts for either option, and Jenn was grateful to talk with someone she trusted. Valerie reassured her that the rewards, though not without sacrifice, were worth any time and expense. By the end of the trip, one option would be clear for Jenn.

I heard snippets of their lengthy discussions but for the most part kept my mouth shut, supplying no comments of my own. I spent my time taking in the fantastic scenery. When Val outlined her intuitions of how our children might be as young adults, my ears perked up. Just as the conversation had been memorable to Jenn, I was intrigued. I wondered if she really envisioned such things or if she was just making them up. I made a mental note to ask her about it later. Either way, her comments made me smile.

Caroline, our traveling companion from France, must have been having a bad day. Her disposition during our ride was less than pleasant. She made snide comments about the cramped conditions, and no matter the subject, she had been there and done that. Even Thomas, our German companion, adamantly disputed several of her comments. Jeff and I were more interested in the sights out our van windows than listening to the conversations.

"Val, look at that lake. Wow, take a picture," I said to Valerie, motioning her to use the camera sitting in her lap. Val rolled her eyes at Jenn and smiled. "Val, that's really beautiful. Did you get the shot?" I repeated. "Did you see that road sign? Was that a snake symbol on the warning sign? We should get a photo of that," I said after a few more miles down the road.

"What about the kids and families we've seen along the

way?" Val said. "I should have been taking pictures of them, not some lake or goofy signpost." Valerie leaned over to Jenn. "I think people are more interesting than landscapes."

Jenn smiled back at Val and seemed to know exactly what she was talking about.

At the outskirts of Tikal, the driver stopped the van just off the road, and we piled out to purchase a park entrance pass. We were more than happy to pay our admission fee of just over six US dollars, as it also offered the chance to get out of the cramped van and stretch our legs. Our French companion wasn't so enthusiastic with our payment stop. After three in the afternoon, a Tikal entrance pass was good for not only the current day but the next day as well. Since it was early afternoon, she would need to wait for another ride if she wanted the reduced admission fee. Her little scene of defiance, though strange, was welcomed by the rest of the van's occupants, as it meant she would remain outside the park's border and no longer ride with us.

We loaded back into the van, less one small woman, and immediately the road and scenery became the best we'd seen so far. There was no doubt we were in the jungle. Lush greenery was everywhere, and we completely forgot about the conditions inside the small minivan.

It wasn't long before we reached the end of the road, and our driver dropped us off in a gravel parking lot near the park's main facilities. He strongly suggested he should be the one to pick us up for our return trip. In broken English, he stated something about how difficult it can be to get a ride back and that "some drivers cannot be trusted." We paid him for the ride and thanked him for his service but didn't commit to the return trip, not wanting to encumber our plans with a specific pickup time and hoping a different driver would make the time more enjoyable by providing commentary during the trip.

There were limited accommodations available in Tikal, and we hoped the Jaguar Inn had rooms for us. If not, Jeff had read about some outside hammocks available for visitors. As necessary, those would become our beds for the night. Fortunately, two bungalows were available. Jeff and Jenn requested the room set farthest back on the property, and Val and I took the remaining room.

"Hey, Rod, let's see if they have Internet access here. We should send a message to the kids. I miss them already," Val said on the way to the bungalow.

"Okay, sure. Good idea," I replied, having somewhat forgotten about contacting the children. "I'm sure they're having fun with Grandma and Grandpa," I continued, trying to sound like I'd been thinking the same thing.

"Let's make sure we contact them tomorrow. I don't know when we'll have the next opportunity to say hi to them," Valerie said.

"Tomorrow for sure," I said, making a promise that, at the time, I had every intention to keep.

We opened the unlocked door to the small duplex-style building and brought our packs inside the modestly appointed and seemingly clean room. There were two beds on the right-hand side of the room, one a single and the other a three-quarter bed, though hardly distinguishable from the single.

At the far end of the room was a bathroom with a small shower. A small nightstand and a narrow rug occupied the space between the two beds.

"This will work for a while," I said. Val nodded and continued inspecting the room. It felt good to have a place we could unpack our belongings and call ours, even if only for less than twenty-four hours.

I noticed two hammocks on the open porch just outside the door, and they looked more than a little inviting. *I just need to get something to read first,* I thought.

We had purchased several travel books for the trip, but I hadn't had a chance to thoroughly read them beforehand. Since I was a wise and seasoned traveler (at least in my own mind), I'd cut out selected sections from the guidebooks that I felt were relevant to our trip. This technique allowed the bulk of the books' pages to remain at home while providing essential information and the least amount of weight in our packs. I opened my pack and searched for the portions on Tikal.

As I looked for the small set of stapled pages, I smiled and shook my head. Finding the document wasn't easy among all the fins, snorkels and masks dominating my backpack. Worrying over the weight of paper seemed silly now, and I questioned my earlier assessment of being a seasoned traveler. With the contents of my pack strewn about, I found the pages of my personalized travel books and headed for the hammocks.

Swinging from side to side three feet off the ground, engrossed in the pages, I learned that the place where we now resided was considered a magical place and one of the best on earth.

*How great is this?!* Mayan ruins were just a short hike away from our very spot. The more I read, the more eager I became to trek farther into the jungle and see this ancient world for myself.

"Val, are you ready to go?" I asked, awkwardly getting out of the hammock.

"Yep, I'll be ready in a minute. I'm sure Jeff and Jenn will be coming by soon," she replied.

The hike to reach the innermost temple complex took much longer than we'd anticipated. The park didn't seem very busy, and given the time of day, we were not surprised that the traffic was heading in the opposite direction and out of the park. Most of the conversations we overheard were not in English, the predominant language seeming to be German.

Walking among the ancient ruins was, well, indeed magical. The temples rose seamlessly and effortlessly from the earth. In several places, the heavily weathered structures were indistinguishable from the jungle itself. The gripping blend of multiple shades of green coupled with aged, gray stone was striking. The absence of any particular route, markers, descriptions of the stone figures, guided tours or other tourists made the time even more mysterious and special.

We climbed several of the structures, and as we sat atop the pyramid-shaped creations, the once-vibrant kingdom seemed to be calling to itself. The sensation was unmistakable. From our vantage point high in the rain forest canopy, we could hear the unremitting screeching of howler monkeys. Their ear-piercing notes, almost deafening at times, only added to what was a wonderfully strange and extraordinary place.

After taking in all we could, the four of us headed back to our rooms. We hadn't yet acclimated to the climate, and the bright sun and high heat had drained our energy. We needed to replenish ourselves if we were to return to the temples later that evening to experience one of the highly anticipated parts of the trip.

"Hey, look," said Jeff, pointing to the edge of the building near the visitor's center.

Just in front of us was a brownish-gray animal roughly the size of a raccoon. The animal's face and particularly its snout were elongated, and it had a long, narrow tail with alternating color bands. It looked at us for a moment, then kept walking along the edge of the building.

"That's cool," was my inspirational and intelligent comeback. "I've seen this animal before in a zoo or on TV. What is it called?"

"I'm pretty sure it's a type of coati," Jeff replied.

The day continued to treat us to exceptional surprises and beauty. With a little rest, some food in our stomachs and great anticipation, we prepared to make the trek back into the ruins. The day's main event was to view the sunset from atop Temple IV in the far western portion of Tikal.

A little after 5:00 p.m., we made our way back into the dense forest and past the ruins we'd climbed earlier in the day. Our ground-level vantage point obscured our ability to discern with any real accuracy how fast the sun was descending. Our surroundings were getting darker, and it didn't help our anxiety when someone going in the opposite direction said, "You'd better hurry or you'll miss the sunset."

Power-walking now, we moved through an area that seemed much different than it had appeared just a few hours ago. The tall trees cast long, dark shadows across the landscape. The temples looked much broader and taller with the sun hitting them at an oblique angle rather than from directly overhead. Large oropendola birds sounded continuously, flocks of them gathering in their hanging nests high above our heads. The contrast between this movement and our earlier visit added to the mysteriousness of the forest.

Rounding a corner along the trail, we saw a large temple towering through the trees in front of us.

"That has to be Temple IV," Jenn said.

"I sure hope it is," Val said, taking in the temple's grandeur.

"We're fine. We'll make it," Jeff said with his no-worries attitude.

From the temple's large base, the climb to the summit didn't appear strenuous, though that was only a visual deception. Our opinion changed by the time we reached the top. The vigorous ascent took us to a plateau that encircled the structure near the temple's summit, and we understood why this was one of the more prominent temples.

Our momentous day of starting in another country, making the necessary connections along the way, and reaching the temple's apex added to the feeling of accomplishment. The day had been exhausting, but the efforts put a smile on my face and provided a feeling of fulfillment.

We reached the top in plenty of time to see the sunset and joined several other people who had made the pilgrimage. We greeted one another with smiles and nods, as English wasn't the common language among us.

The view was spectacular. We were well above the rain forest's canopy, and lush green jungle spread out in all directions as far as the eye could see. The sky was clear and sun-filled, the temperature near ninety degrees. As the sun descended into the western horizon, it cast an acute yellowish hue upon everything in its path, distorting the landscape with long dark shrouds of shadows. I felt privileged to be there.

We tried to capture the splendor on our video camera and in photographs, but we knew the resulting images would not portray its magical wonder. A fellow traveler sitting next to us suggested the four of us gather for a group photo. We gladly accepted his offer, as our photographs rarely included all four of us at the same time.

The photo was a great portrait of our time together, though another photo stands out amid the rest. Just before the sunset's finale, several hundred yards to our left, we noticed a white tree with red leaves among a sea of green. The sun had illuminated, as if purposefully, this singular tree in the jungle below.

"Rod, that's a nice shot," Val said, pointing to the tree and suggesting I take the photo.

"I was just going to say the same thing to you. Here, take the camera, Val. You're the better photographer." Val moved our 35mm SLR camera to her right eye and pushed the button.

"I think I got it," Val said, handing me the camera. Indeed she had. The picture, which currently rests prominently on my bedroom dresser, not only captured the exceptional moment but serves as a precious reminder of how a little thing two people share can make a lasting impression.

The experience was everything we had hoped it would be; however, the physical setting of the sun wasn't the spectacular and inspiring part. *I've seen better sunsets,* I thought. The magic was in the place and in the closeness we all felt at that very moment. The sun sets every day. Yet not every day does one sit atop an ancient ruin built by a once-powerful Mayan civilization long since departed. It was a complex mixture of historical significance, geographic setting, architecture, nature, and, at its very essence, the connection between these features and one's own presence that made it magnificent.

Jeff, who had also traveled to many wonderful places on this earth, would later record his feeling of the moment in his journal: "It doesn't get much better than this."

We let others make their exits first, as we were in no particular hurry to get back. Since we were the last group, two additional individuals accompanied us. The men were park rangers of sorts, with matching uniforms and pistol-grip .12-gauge shotguns slung across their shoulders. This image seemed very out of place, with us fresh off our "kumbaya" sunset experience. Nevertheless, the display commanded our attention.

The taller of the park's rangers was notably nervous about our dillydallying and nodded and motioned us along. He was clearly eager to get back to the park compound as soon as possible. We'd heard of bandits in the area, and tourists on a small jungle trail at night would be easy prey if not for the rangers' firepower. The other uniform-clad fellow was less anxious and chatted away, practicing his English and providing us a personal tour during the walk back.

Our small band separated for a time as Jeff escorted a group of sunset watchers along the narrow path, illuminating their way with his headlamp. Jeff frequently made fun of such inexperienced folks without essential know-how or equipment that would be useful on such a trip, yet he always helped them.

Blackness now replaced the afternoon's inviting greenery, and unusual sounds and silhouetted movements of the jungle's creatures captured our attention. The birds had transformed from simply beautiful to peculiarly disconcerting as their elongated shaggy black basket nests swayed unnaturally against the lighter-colored western skyline. Above our heads, the abrupt and ever-shifting movements of monkeys in the trees added to the eeriness. We became grateful for the accompaniment of our ranger companions.

"Where's Jeff and his headlamp when you need him?" Val asked.

"I have mine," said Jenn, but before she could retrieve it, our personal tour guide took out his flashlight and grinned.

A little farther along the stimulating path, we encountered yet another spectacular sight, as we unexpectedly found ourselves in a swarm of fireflies. They appeared en masse, seemingly from nowhere, and when we turned off our headlamps and flashlight, the giant chartreuse insects surrounded us, blinking on and off like a million mini stars in every direction. Val in particular loved this. The unforgettable moment of walking through the jungle at night with a million twinkling lights comes rushing back to me every time I see a firefly. I now have a soft spot in my heart for any bioluminescent winged beetle.

*I should capture this on video,* I thought, wondering why I hadn't been recording the entire time. "Hey, guys, wait up. Let me get some of this on the video camera."

"It's too dark. I'm not sure you will get much," Valerie said.

"I know. There is a twilight mode, if I can figure out how to use it."

I found what I believed was the night setting on the camera and recorded some footage. I couldn't know then the significance it would hold for me in the future.

The trail widened, and soon we reached the visitor center. The park rangers said good-bye and turned down another path as we continued to our bungalows. I desperately needed a shower—either warm or cold water would do—a change of clothes, something to drink, and a meal. The generators would turn off at nine whether we were ready or not, so we needed to move quickly.

Jeff and Jenn had already grabbed some food by the time we met up with them, and we joined them at a small table outside our room. We had a couple of Guatemalan beers, strangely enough called Famosa "Gallo" beer, which, upon hearing Jeff's translation of *gallo*—rooster—I secretly wondered if chicken parts were among its ingredients.

Sitting by the picnic table, we reflected on the incredible things we'd done and the amazing sights we'd seen over the past thirty-two hours and those we had planned for the next day. I was happy, and so was the rest of our little crew.

"Let's take some pictures of us relaxing after our adventure," Val said.

"Okay, smile," I said. As Jenn, Jeff and Val turned toward the camera smiling, so did I.

The experience of taking this photo was similar to many others just like it. There was no foreshadowing of events yet to unfold later that night. No suggestions, signs or indications in what was now the coolness of the jungle's night air that one of us had just smiled for the camera for the very last time.

# PART II

*Instantaneous Change*

# Chapter 7

## *The Awakening*

W e'd moved our mini party inside the restaurant so Val and I could get something to eat. As we finished eating, the electric lights went off as we'd expected. The server lit the two candles that were already sitting atop the table, and the gentle glow and subtle movements of candlelight on our faces only enhanced the ambiance. Our conversation was engaging, and Valerie was enjoying her time away from her otherwise on-the-go life. We were one of the last groups to leave the restaurant, laughing with each step.

"That was nice," Val said as we entered our room.

"What was?" I said.

"I don't know—the day. Traveling, the ruins, hanging out

with Jenn and Jeff, the sunset, meeting new people—just everything," she replied. "I'm really tired, though. We should gather the supplies we need for the morning."

To complete our Tikal experience, we'd decided during dinner to get up before sunrise and make our way back into the ruins, climb the temple again and watch the dawning of a new day above the jungle's canopy. We'd read and heard from others during the trip that the sunrise was often better than the sunset, so we wanted to experience it for ourselves.

"I'll set my watch. What time did we say we would meet Jeff and Jenn?" I asked.

"We settled on just before five. I'm sure they'll be up and waiting for us. We should plan on being up at four thirty just to be safe."

"Okay, we're set. I'll put it here on the stand," I said, placing my well-worn, Velcro-strapped wristwatch on the nightstand between the two beds.

Though we hadn't spent a lot of time in our small room, we were comfortable in it. We had our choice of sleeping separately, as neither of the beds was very large, but without hesitation, we both crawled into the slightly larger of the two beds.

*What's causing all the commotion?* I thought, half awake, listening to muffled voices and someone coughing in the adjoining room.

"They must be getting up to catch the sunrise as well," I said quietly, not knowing if Valerie had heard the noises. *I can't believe it's time to get up already. What a fast night's sleep.*

"Hmm, yeah, they're up early," Val replied slowly. "Sorry, I'm in the middle of the bed. I'll move over so you're not against the wall."

"I'm fine. You don't need to," I said, not minding our closeness.

"What time is it? Val, can you grab my watch? It's on the nightstand next to you." I could hear her fumbling for the watch through the collection of water bottles, guidebooks, and heavily soiled quetzals. When the second water bottle toppled from the nightstand to the floor, I chuckled and wondered why she was having such difficulty finding the watch.

"The watch should be there. I remember placing it in the middle of the table," I said, knowing that navigating the table's obstacles in darkness was likely encumbering her efforts.

"Here it is," Val said, handing me the watch.

"It's only 2:50," I said after pressing the small button on the right side of the watch that illuminated the numbers. "It's not time to get up yet." I was a little upset that we were now almost fully awake in the middle of the night but also relieved we had some additional time to sleep. I handed the watch back to Val, and she replaced it on the nightstand.

"I'm not feeling well," Val said, repositioning herself in the middle of the bed and moving her shoulders back and forth between the sheets.

*I'm not feeling the best either, now that you mention it. My stomach feels a little weird,* I thought without saying anything to Valerie, assuming she was also talking about her stomach. A combination of jet lag, hiking all day, eating unfamiliar food, restlessness from the noise next door and anticipation for our morning's adventure was likely the cause of our discomfort.

Repositioning my head on the pillow, I noticed Valerie

appeared to be sleeping once again. My mind flashed through the sights and sounds of the previous day, and just as quickly, the thoughts drifted from my mind and I was asleep.

I heard a noise coming from Valerie. It sounded like a release of air propelled through her mouth. From my deep sleep, I was instantly awake and continued listening. Within a fraction of a second, I heard a sound that was similar to the first, and I realized Val was having another one of her nightmares.

Val's involuntary night wakings had become more frequent over the past few years and were not from your average nightmares. They seemed all too real, too harsh, and I had become keen to their patterns. The nightmares typically followed a similar progression: starting out as just slightly heavier breathing but then becoming deeper and louder, closer and closer to hyperventilation, many times causing her to jolt upright in bed. Even in the deepest sleep, my body had become proficient in recognizing the earliest signs, and I would wake at the first sound of an episode. I often needed to call out, "Val . . . Val . . . Valerie . . . Valerie . . ." And many times I had to grab her trembling body before she would finally wake and regain herself. She would look me in the eyes, seemingly unaware of what had just happened.

The nightmares were unnerving, even frightening at times. Val could seldom recall the specific details other than someone had tried to get her or the kids and that the dream was violently cruel. The sporadic events became an unwelcome visitor for both Valerie and me.

Yet something was different this time. There was no thrashing of her body, and the noise of air passing from her mouth remained constant, neither increasing nor getting softer.

"Val . . . Val," I said. I moved my arms out from under the sheets and grabbed her right arm. There was only the slightest moan, followed by a gasp of breath.

"What's going on?" *Okay, this is not a nightmare; something's wrong,* I thought as I started to move to Val's other side. "Valerie, Valerie, what's wrong? Can you hear me? Valerie." I continued calling her name as I removed the thin blanket and sheet that covered her and moved my body across hers. I was now standing between the two beds and the small nightstand. The process of freeing her body from beneath the covers generated a strange sensation that caught me by surprise. Val had no reaction to my touch. As I slightly moved her body, she seemed to be completely relaxed. Her lack of movement was awkward, and I struggled to figure out what was happening.

I noticed a water bottle at my feet. *Maybe this will help.* I grabbed and opened it. I poured some water out of the bottle into the palm of my right hand and splashed it around her face and mouth. There was no response other than a slight gurgling sound from some water entering Val's airway.

The sound was startling. My body instantly tingled, my senses amplified—a combination of fear and instinct now in control. I quickly moved her body on its side to make sure there was no longer water in her mouth. "Val, what's wrong? What's wrong, Val?" I asked, thinking she might be able to hear me. There was no response to my words or my touch, only the expelling of air and a slight moan. Fifteen to twenty seconds had passed since the first sound from Valerie that had woken me, and I knew something more serious was happening.

I moved her head to the right, curled over her body, and swiped her mouth with my index finger, checking for any foreign material interfering with her breathing. My movements were instinctive, yet the process of placing my fingers in Val's mouth was unsettling. Her body was warm and limp. Her joints were loose but her body heavy. She gave no resistance to my moving her, as gravity appeared to be the only law working on her body.

I had never encountered such a situation before. I was disconcerted, though I knew I needed to push the strange feeling out of my mind. My mind raced. I was alert and was experiencing a heightened state of consciousness.

We were inside a building in the middle of the night without electricity or lights—the generator had turned off long ago. Yet I felt I could see everything I needed to and chose not to grab my headlamp.

Approximately forty-five seconds had passed since I'd woken to Valerie's strange breathing. I straightened my body from its bent position over Val and, for a brief second, thought about my next move.

"Jeff!" I yelled twice in the general direction of the open window behind the bed. I didn't know where Jeff and Jenn's bungalow was, and I didn't think yelling would accomplish much, but I needed to yell. There was a chance they'd hear me, so shouting Jeff's name was worth a try.

*Could this be a possible allergic reaction to a bite? Yeah, yeah, maybe from a snake, spider or some kind of lizard. Think,*

*think* . . . I tried to recall travel books and talks with other travelers about potentially hazardous animals or insects in the area. I remembered that some venomous threats existed but were very uncommon. *Still, it could be,* I thought, as I moved her body from side to side looking for bite marks on her skin.

"Light, I need more light," I said fervently, looking at the other bed. I turned and grabbed my headlamp and continued to look for evidence of a bite. Nothing.

*Maybe it's a reaction to the food? Yes, that must be it, but I think we all ate roughly the same thing. What did Val eat that was different? It doesn't matter now. I'll think about that later.*

*The sound is coming from her throat; maybe she's choking on something,* I thought once again as I ran my fingers along the inside of her mouth for the second time. Nothing.

*If air is still being expelled from her mouth, and since there is still some sound coming from her throat, there must be some other issue.* I continued my meager diagnosis. I noticed Valerie's eyelids were three-quarters open and her eyes somewhat rolled back in her head, their color less bright than normal. I didn't know what that meant, but it emphasized the severity of the situation. Simply waking Valerie up from some sort of deep sleep no longer seemed possible.

I noticed she was only in a nightshirt and panties. Since I would most certainly not be the only person seeing Val tonight, I thought she would prefer to have some shorts on. I grabbed the first pair I could find and put them on her. I needed more clothes as well and spotted the shorts I'd worn the day before and put them on. Turning to grab a shirt, I saw the clean pair of shorts I'd set out to watch the sunrise. "Not important," I said to myself.

I needed to get Val off the bed and onto a hard surface, as the bed was not conducive to what I was about to start. I pushed the other bed against the opposite wall, making as much room as possible on the floor. The narrow rug between the two beds, dirty or not, would have to suffice.

Turning Val slightly on her side and pushing my arms underneath her, I simultaneously lifted and pulled her from the bed. I tried to hold her head steady as we moved to the floor; however, in the process, her arm moved from across her body, striking hard against the floor. I inhaled, and my eyes widened; the sight and sound of the brief event caught me off guard. It was clear Val no longer had control of her body.

By the time I'd checked Val's body for signs of an external wound and moved her to the floor, another forty-five seconds to a minute had passed. I checked for a pulse. *Yes, a slight one maybe . . . no, maybe not. Dammit, I can't tell.*

I believed Val needed assistance breathing, and once I started CPR, I didn't want to quit. *Time to get help.* Valerie and I needed Jenn and Jeff's assistance.

# Chapter 8

## Desperate for Help

---

Jeff awoke to what sounded like a voice yelling in the distance. Amid the otherwise inherent sounds of the night's dense air, there it was for a second time. It almost sounded like someone calling his name.

"Jenn, are you awake?" Jeff asked.

"Yes. It's only 3:17 in the morning. It's not time to get up yet," Jenn replied. "What's going on outside?

"From the noise of the howlers, I would guess they scared someone nearby," Jeff said.

Jenn recalled reading that howler monkeys are typically active at or just before dawn. It seemed too early for monkeys to be making the noise.

"It's bandits. Oh my God, someone is robbing the place," Jenn said.

I ran from the room yelling Jenn's and Jeff's names. My instinct was to turn left, thinking they'd gone in that general direction after saying good night.

Though I was panicked, my emotions were not completely out of control. I knew something terrible had happened to Valerie, but I just needed help getting her conscious again.

"Jeff . . . Jenn . . . Jennifer, Jeff!" I yelled, repeating the names into the night sky, making myself known to all—whether they cared to listen or not.

"Rod, we're here. What's going on?" came a voice from inside a building somewhere in the distance.

"Something's wrong with Valerie. Please come quick," I yelled in the general direction of the voice and began running back to the room.

"Rod, what's wrong?" Jenn yelled.

"I don't know. Val's in trouble," I yelled over my shoulder, sprinting back to the room.

There was no change in Val's condition as I reentered the room. She was lying motionless on the floor in the exact position I had left her thirty seconds earlier. I got on my knees next to her left side and again checked for a pulse on the side of her throat and on her wrist. Her eyes, still rolled slightly into the tops of her eyelids, did not move. I touched her face with my hands in hopes my touch would change their position. "You'll be all right, Val. You'll be okay. Can you hear me?"

Seconds later, I heard Jeff and Jenn coming toward me, and within moments, light from their headlamps filled the room.

"Oh my God," Jenn said, seeing Val now lying on the floor between the beds. "What happened?"

"I don't know. She just started to gasp for air. I need to

start CPR. Please go get help. We need help," I said to Jenn without looking at her.

"Do you know how to do that?" she asked.

"Yes, yes, Val needs help. Please go and get some help," I said, this time making eye contact with Jenn. Without hesitation, Jenn left the room. Jeff helped me check for a pulse, and although it was very weak, we believed she had one. I briefly checked again for obvious signs of bites or stings and found none.

Less than four minutes had passed since I'd first heard the sounds come from Val's mouth. Not knowing the cause of Valerie's condition was hard to accept, but trying to figure it out wasn't helping the situation either.

I began CPR with a reasonable amount of confidence. I was trained, many times, in fact, to do what I was about to do, though there was a strong sense of how very different this was from any training. I started chest compressions. "One and two and three and four and . . ." *I think it's fifteen and two. Fifteen chest compressions, then two rescue breaths. Right or wrong, that's what I'm going to use,* I thought, finding it difficult to concentrate on such details. After I said the number fifteen, I breathed into her mouth. Again, I counted aloud to fifteen and gave two more rescue breaths.

I started to get a rhythm to the CPR, and as I continued, I reflected on instructors discussing the role of oxygen in the body and how crucial it is to the brain. *Is it a matter of a minute, ten minutes, or longer before it starts to affect the brain?* I wasn't sure, and I didn't dwell on it long. I was manually pumping blood through Valerie's heart and breathing air into her lungs; everything would be okay.

"It will be okay, Val. We will get through this. Just please wake up," I said, talking to Val as I counted in my mind, *seven . . . eight . . . nine . . .* In the background, I thought I could hear Jennifer calling out, but the sound was intermittent and far off. I focused on the task at hand, knowing Jenn would get us the help we needed.

～‿‿‿

Jenn's first stop was the restaurant where we'd been sitting and laughing just a few hours earlier. There was a reasonable chance that workers who could help might be inside. Jenn pounded on the locked door without a response, then she moved to the window, trying to see inside with her headlamp. She yelled and pounded on the glass, knowing that the force of her forearms might very well break it.

"Please help. We need help. Can someone help us?" Jenn yelled. Her questions met only darkness and the reverberations of her own voice. She moved from the restaurant and began knocking on individual doors with the same pleas for help. She received the same response: nothing. Jenn was quickly becoming frustrated; she needed a different approach.

Jenn moved to the next door, her voice now more desperate and pleading rather than simply asking or inquiring. "My friend is in trouble. I will not stop pounding on this door and screaming until you tell me if you or anyone else in your room has medical training. Yes or no—are you a doctor or nurse?"

This time she heard movement inside but no immediate response. Then, "No, we are not medically trained" came the anxious words from the other side of the door. Jenn hurriedly moved to the next door and got a similar result: no assistance. The respondents' voices became more fearful as Jenn went along. She wondered if they, too, had heard the frightening sounds just moments before I'd called out her name. If Jenn had thought bandits were looking to rob or harm them, maybe others did as well. With this realization, she ran back to the room where Jeff and I were attending to Valerie.

"Any change?" Jenn asked, rushing into the bungalow. Jeff was the only one who even noticed Jenn was back in the room.

A shake of Jeff's head and a faint no were all Jenn received.

Jenn looked at Val, who was motionless, barely breathing, lying in the middle of the hard floor. Bitter thoughts entered her mind. She suspected Val's condition must have been from a bite and a resulting allergic reaction, and for Jenn, there was no doubt that she'd caused this. Seeing Val on the floor a second time only intensified her feelings that she was to blame.

Jenn moved to Jeff and shook her head. "We never even asked them which room they wanted; we just took the farthest room. We wanted to be the most rugged travelers of the group. They had no choice, and now Val got bitten in the room we made them take. We were so stupid to do that."

I finally noticed Jenn out of the corner of my eye as I kept up my counting and compressions. "Did you find any help? We need help."

CPR was my primary focus, though on several occasions, my arm started to quiver when I thought about the situation. I told myself I needed resolve, I needed to be strong. If I could keep Val alive and get to a hospital, she would be okay, and if that was what the situation demanded, then that was what I would do.

"Jenn, is anyone able to help?" I asked in the direction of her voice, but she was once again out the door.

Jenn had a renewed sense of urgency and a feeling of desperation. More people answered her persistent calls for help, maybe realizing her shouting would not cease until they responded. Unfortunately, neither doctors nor any other medically trained personal were among them. Thinking an anaphylactic allergic reaction required medicine such as epinephrine to reverse its symptoms, Jenn and a few other travelers, now out of their rooms, started to yell for an auto-injector. "My friend is having an allergic reaction. Does anyone have an epi-injector? We need an epi-injector," Jenn shouted in the direction of yet another door.

The outside hammocks available for travelers not sleeping in rooms were nearby. Caroline, the woman from France with whom we'd shared the van ride the day before, happened to be sleeping on one of them. She immediately grasped the situation and the urgent need for medical assistance, showing none of her earlier unpleasant attitude.

"We'll go to the Tikal Inn and see if we can find help there," Caroline told Jenn in English with her French accent.

"Do you know where the Tikal Inn is?" Jenn asked. She'd heard of another inn close by but hadn't seen it earlier in the day.

Caroline gathered two other women sleeping in the same area and discussed the location of the other inn.

"We believe we can find it," Caroline said.

Jenn urged them not to be fussy regarding whom they could find to help—anyone with some medical training would have more experience than we did. Caroline and her newly formed team courageously started running through the trees with only the small lights from their headlamps bobbing and flashing in front of them. Jenn watched them disappear into the jungle's density. Their sounds faded first, and then their lights darkened in the distance.

"Godspeed," Jenn said to herself. With the women out of sight, Jenn felt alone, and a disconcerting feeling overcame her.

Jeff remained with Val and me, providing moral support and light from his headlamp. For the most part, I had not completely panicked. I was doing what I thought was needed for Val. My mind, however, was in another world—full of random scenarios of what else we could do. *I looked for signs of a possible cause of Val's condition, I'm performing CPR, Jenn is trying to get help . . . what else can we do? What we really need is a hospital. Jenn will find someone to help.* I was certain we would revive Val from her current condition.

Even with this confidence, I realized Val might not be the same again, having been deprived of oxygen for so long. She might not be able to do some of the things she was accustomed to and there was a possibility that she would have extra needs or be handicapped in some way.

*Eight . . . nine . . . ten . . .* My mind still counted each stroke.

I would, without a doubt, take care of her, whatever the outcome. We would be together, and that was all that really mattered. The possibility of a permanent exodus did not enter my mind.

To my left, I noticed other people standing in my room and soon thereafter more people filling the room. I recognized three of them from the adjacent bungalow, but most of the people I had never seen before. They were simply looking down at us in disbelief. I neither asked who they were nor cared. I continued to compress Val's chest and supply air to her lungs.

As Jenn continued to wake everyone at the Jaguar Inn, she caught a glimpse of several spots of light appearing from the darkness. Caroline and her two friends, accompanied by four other people, rushed toward her. "You found help," Jenn called to Caroline, who had been shouting *"Docteur, médecin, médecin"* for the last one hundred yards. Caroline simply nodded her head, out of breath.

"Rod, we found doctors. Doctors are here. They can help," Jenn shouted, running back into the room.

I had no immediate reaction, although, based on the reaction of the crowd in my room, I should have been ecstatic. My repetitive task and focus on Valerie tuned out most of the surroundings so I was oblivious to what Jenn was saying. Out of the corner of my eye, I noticed three men toss the bed on which Val and I had been sleeping minutes ago on its side, slamming it against the wall. Something new was happening in the room, but I wasn't sure what the commotion was exactly. I noticed people speaking a language I hadn't heard earlier— definitely not English, nor did it sound like Spanish. I could not place it, but after short consideration, it slipped from my mind as I continued resuscitation.

One of the people in the room motioned me to stop CPR. I simply shook my head and gave Val two rescue breaths.

"What happened?" said a relatively young-looking man with a strong accent, positioning himself on his knees on Valerie's opposite side, where the bed used to be.

"I'm not sure. I woke up to the sounds of her expelling air and gasping for breath," I replied without looking up. Various conversations in many languages now flooded the room.

*French. These people are from France, I suddenly realized.*

It meant nothing, however, as all the other sounds were just a mixture of noises. The man opposite me motioned me for a second time to stop CPR.

*Why should I stop? Ridiculous. Doesn't he know you should not start and stop CPR?* I looked up hoping to find Jeff in the room. Upon seeing him, I gave a slight upward and sideways nod, hoping he would understand my sign for "Get these people out of our way."

"They're doctors, Rod. They can help," was Jeff's response.

I heard Jeff's words, but my mind was slow to comprehend his message. *Doctors—Jenn located doctors. Out here in the jungle. So soon? Doctors in the room?* I couldn't push the CPR sequence from my thoughts, so I kept pumping. The young Frenchman reached over Val and lightly touched my arm to get my attention. I looked up from Valerie and into his eyes.

"I can help," he said.

"Rod, these are French doctors," Jenn stated, noticing my hesitancy.

Two others had now joined the young male doctor and me on the floor. Another man, slightly larger and older than the other, and a young woman, whom I assumed was French as well. The newcomers to the floor looked confident but scared. At their insistence, I stopped CPR and straightened my back. The young man began to speak rapidly in French.

"Jenn, we need to get to a hospital," I said, turning my head in the direction I'd heard Jenn's voice just moments ago, but she wasn't there.

"We're going to get more help," I heard trailing off from outside the doorway. I wasn't sure how far the nearest hospital was, but we needed real medical assistance, quickly.

The three of them examined Val's body, talking rapidly in their native language—I understood none of it. They checked her eyes, moving her eyelids up and down. They checked for a pulse, then, shockingly, one of them gave a sudden slap to Valerie's face, then another. They yelled at her to wake up. The sudden change in tactics seemed harsh and unnecessary and was only a warm-up to what came next.

Without warning, the young doctor raised his arm, clenched his fist tightly, and forcefully thrust it into Valerie's chest. The violent act caught me completely off guard. Valerie's body collapsed around the blow, and her extremities shook upon impact and then quickly resumed a limp position. The young doctor yelled again at Valerie to respond, then again slammed his clenched fist into her chest. This disturbed me like nothing had so far. I knew, or thought I knew, that the purpose of the powerful blows was to shock, reset or restart her heart, but that didn't make it any easier to watch.

Valerie lay motionless on the floor, the same position I'd placed her in earlier. A person I had never met, in wrinkled street clothes, speaking a foreign language, whom a young woman sleeping in a hammock in the jungle told us was a doctor, was suddenly, forcefully striking my wife's body with his fist.

After three powerful blows, I couldn't bear it anymore.

"Okay, that's enough," I said.

The pounding stopped, and they began administering CPR immediately. I don't know if my uneasiness of not knowing anything about their medical backgrounds had any bearing on my questioning their CPR techniques, but I did notice their method was different from mine. *Maybe this is a better way,* I thought, trusting some inner sense.

Time seemed to move in slow motion. My body felt numb, while my mind was keen to what was happening around me. The sight and sound of people slapping Valerie and thumping her chest were beyond disturbing. I needed to trust these doctors. I needed to believe, or maybe just wanted to believe, they would be able to help Val.

"We've located an ambulance. It's on its way," Jenn said, breathlessly entering the room.

This time I not only heard her voice, I understood the significance of the words, and they were unbelievable. "Excellent. An ambulance is on the way." For the second time in twenty minutes, I felt renewed hope and optimism, and it was tremendous. *First, three doctors just happened to be in Tikal during our stay—what great luck. Now an ambulance is on its way. Fantastic.* This would not be the last time what seemed like excellent news would temporarily buoy our spirits.

"It's working. The CPR is working," I said, not knowing if the words actually came out of my mouth. I looked at Jenn, and she seemed to sense it as well. For the second time since the French doctors had begun performing CPR, Val's eyes seemed to move slightly downward, and a different noise came from her throat.

"Was that a breath?" Jenn asked.

"I think I feel a pulse," I said, moving my hand from her wrist to her throat.

The possible breakthrough was inspiring, and as the faint sound of an ambulance siren grew louder, so did our optimism.

# Chapter 9

## *It's Already Here*

New faces appeared in the room each time I looked up. People seemed to be coming and going, and most were not speaking English and most looked relatively young. At 3:40 a.m. on a Saturday, it all felt surreal.

"It's here," said a voice from outside the doorway, followed by squeaking vehicle brakes. The sound prompted a quick exodus from the room.

I didn't know where the ambulance came from or how it got there so quickly, and I didn't question its presence. The French doctors did not tell me everything would be okay, or that the slight improvements we saw in Valerie meant we were out of danger, but it seemed they were very pleased to see the ambulance. The roller coaster of emotions was on an upswing.

I moved from my kneeling position for the first time since calling for Jeff and Jenn. "Excuse me," I said, pushing my way to the narrow table across from the overturned beds, looking for our packs. There was no time to consider what might be helpful in the ambulance, and beyond, but three items came to my mind.

Reaching into my daypack, I grabbed my wallet, and then dug into the larger travel pack to get our passports. I turned back to the middle of the room, again excusing myself as I moved past people to look for the third item on my list. "Where's my watch?" I said to myself, looking on the nightstand. My eyes darted back and forth several times, scanning its surface. "Has anyone seen . . ." I started to say, when a shout caught my attention.

"Oxygen!" yelled the female French doctor from the doorway to Jenn, who was standing alongside the ambulance approximately thirty-five yards away.

"Hurry, get the stretcher," someone else called out.

The room became a flurry of activity and filled with a complex mix of words I did not understand. Just after a group of people pulled out the stretcher from between the double doors of the ambulance, Jenn climbed inside to grab the oxygen.

I heard the crackle of a two-way radio and someone talking wildly to the person on the other end of the line. The paramedics did not enter the room; they must have stayed in the ambulance preparing for the trip to the emergency room. I wanted to ask them where the ambulance was from and which emergency room we were going to, but I would have time to ask later.

The people who had run from the room to meet the ambulance were now back with a stretcher. Not wanting to discontinue

CPR, we lifted Val from the floor to the stretcher with the aid of the rug she was on in one quick motion, barely missing a compression. With the first downstroke, it was clear the stretcher had very little rigidity, and we quickly glanced around the room looking for anything to help support Valerie's back. Nothing was obvious, and we needed to go. At least three others grabbed a portion of the stretcher, and we rushed out the door. Halfway to the vehicle, the French doctor motioned us to stop. He administered a few more chest compressions and then nodded, indicating we should proceed to the ambulance.

A portion of the path to the waiting ambulance was a narrow, elevated stone walkway that cut through a small rock garden. As we began moving Valerie again, my open-toed shoe smashed against a rock. The pain instantly moved from my foot to my brain. Under any other circumstance, I would have grabbed my toe, hopped on one foot, and started cursing. In this case, it would be another twenty-one hours before I even remembered the incident.

The ambulance and its bright lights shone in stark contrast to the night's darkness, and while the sound of its arrival had been comforting, the vehicle's physical appearance was exhilarating. The ambulance was full-size, the real deal.

We positioned the stretcher at the foot of the ambulance door, and one of the French doctors called out, "*Un, deux, trois.*" Though the specific words were unfamiliar to many, we all understood their meaning as we lifted Valerie and the stretcher off the ground. As Val's body started through the ambulance door, the ambulance driver must have interpreted the French signals differently because he pushed the vehicle's accelerator, lurching the ambulance forward.

"Stop . . . Stop!" rang out in multiple languages. Just as suddenly, the vehicle jolted to a stop—banging Valerie and the stretcher against the ground.

*How could they think we were ready to take off?* I thought, not believing what had just happened.

We regained our balance and lifted Valerie into the ambulance. I stepped into the vehicle looking to speak with the medics, but as I moved around to Valerie's side, the only other person in the vehicle was heading in the opposite direction toward the rear door.

"Hey," I said, half saying hello and half asking, *Why are you leaving?* I guessed he was going to prepare some medicine or get some additional equipment. I wasn't sure if I should restart CPR, but with no one else in the ambulance besides the driver, I began chest compressions and rescue breathing. *Didn't Jenn yell for oxygen? Where is the oxygen? Is that what the paramedic went to get?*

"We can take more," the paramedic said in Spanish to the dozen or more people gathered near the back of the ambulance. There was no immediate response.

"You have to go with them," Jenn said to the two French doctors who'd taken lead roles in the situation. "Please don't let him go alone. Please, they need you!"

The doctors exchanged no words, just eye contact. They wouldn't have known where their involvement would lead them. They were on holiday, not on call with the hospital. Within an instant of their glances, they grabbed the outside handrail and climbed in.

As I continued chest compressions, the female doctor and the younger male doctor positioned themselves on the bench next to me. *Excellent,* I thought. Not only did we have the medics but also the French doctors along for our trip to the hospital.

"*Podemos tomar otra persona,*" stated the emergency technician to the group of people outside the ambulance, informing them that we could take another person.

Jeff turned to Jenn. "Jenn, you go. I can take care of things here."

Looking down the length of Val's body toward the rear door, I saw Jenn climbing into the ambulance.

I must have looked surprised. "Jeff will find us. I'm not sure where the hospital is, but he'll find it," Jenn assured me.

The back doors to the ambulance closed sometime around 3:45 a.m., and we sped away on the bumpy gravel road.

As large as the ambulance appeared from the outside, it felt considerably smaller with seven adults inside. The early-morning ambulance crew consisted of two male paramedics. One of the men was the driver who had mistakenly taken off before Val was inside the vehicle. The other, the one who had solicited other riders, now stood in the opening between the cab and the back of the ambulance.

*Why aren't you scrambling to help us? We are in the ambulance. Let's get going!*

We may have missed one or two rounds of rescue breathing during the transition, but no more than that. The doctor who had taken control in the room motioned to me that he would like to conduct the chest compressions. After a second indication, I moved in front of Val, and he took over.

With our attention focused on renewed resuscitation, the siren and road noise gave us little chance of hearing the paramedic's questions. He motioned to the driver, and the noise from the siren ceased.

"Is she married?" asked the man for a third time in a slightly louder voice.

Jenn answered, *"Sí."*

"How old is she?" he asked, speaking directly to Jenn after writing down the first answer on a clipboard.

"I'm not sure. Wait . . . forty. She just turned forty," Jenn replied.

I didn't understand the complete Spanish translation, and wondered why the medic was asking seemingly nonurgent questions in the middle of a crisis. *We are still doing CPR; why aren't you doing this? You haven't even examined her yet! You are the paramedics—hook up a damn IV, start administering medicine or at least get a breathing bag set up. What the hell are you doing? Do something.*

Though I was aggravated with their lackadaisical efforts, I held back my thoughts.

"We need your help. Please get out your equipment. When are you going to start helping us?" I said. No response.

I'm sure the other three people breathing on their own in the ambulance had already figured it out, but I had not. Though, soon thereafter, I noticed some attributes that had eluded me previously. The person standing in the front had a two-way radio and several worn leather pouches attached to his belt. In one hand he held a brown clipboard with a plain white piece of paper and in the other a worn pencil. There were no stethoscope, medical devices or, for that matter, any medical insignias or paraphernalia of any kind. Tilting my head slightly, I could see the reflection of the driver's eyes in the rearview mirror. He looked scared. Both the driver and the man with the clipboard wore light tan uniforms, the same as the park rangers we'd seen the day before.

The men I thought were trained medical professionals were merely park staff. They likely had limited medical training, if any at all, and they probably knew less about saving a life than we did. From that point on, I knew they would provide no additional assistance in saving Valerie's life. They would simply chauffeur us to our next destination, as yet unknown.

The realization was crushing. How could I have believed that qualified medical professionals had arrived so soon? I'd just assumed the ambulance had come from a nearby hospital, not a garage in Tikal. I felt silly and naïve. I looked at the doctors and at Jenn, and I sensed they already knew that the people in control of the ambulance were not paramedics.

The interior of the box-shaped vehicle contained shelves, drawers and cabinets on the driver's side and a long bench on the other. The doctors, Jenn and I began opening cabinets and drawers, searching for anything we could use. We needed something to help Val other than our hands and personal breath. Each of the drawers and cabinets we opened was empty. We were in complete disbelief.

*We're in an ambulance. How can there be no medical supplies whatsoever?* We reopened drawers numerous times, somehow expecting a different result the second or third time. In our haste, maybe we'd overlooked a drawer, or maybe there was a piece of equipment or a vial of medicine hiding in a far back corner that we'd missed. The two men who came with the ambulance did not stop us from rummaging through their cupboards. They also had no reaction when we showed them the empty drawers and our turned-up hands. The gloriously welcomed ambulance now instantly transformed to nothing more than a glorified van with fancy lights and a siren.

The lack of anything useful prompted an animated conversation between the doctors. Soon their conversation fell silent, and CPR once again became our focus. The rigors of the activity, however, were taking their toll.

To think about the entirety of the situation was exhausting, so I did not dwell on it. A mix of panic and fear churned inside me, but as a group, we did not talk about it. I had hope and could see no signs from the doctors and Jenn that I shouldn't. This was a time to save a life, Valerie's life, and we focused on that task.

Communication among our group included a combination of English, French, and Spanish, a lot of which I did not understand. Signs, gestures and facial expressions made communication possible. For the first time, I learned our French companions' names.

"My name is Ludovic, and this is Julie," stated the male doctor.

I smiled and stated, "My wife's name is Valerie." With this exchange, the situation became more personal than it had been just seconds ago.

"Please hurry. We need to get to a hospital," I said loudly toward the front of the vehicle. The driver and his companion just stared at the scene with a look of utter confusion and disbelief.

I assumed the ambulance crew was taking us to the nearest emergency room, direction and distance unknown. With no medical supplies, we had to get to the hospital soon.

A few days before our trip, I'd done a cursory review of

some guide maps and recalled arrows that referenced distant towns. The ambulance didn't seem to be taking the route we'd traveled to get to Tikal, which seemed to me like a good thing. The areas we'd traveled through yesterday weren't very populated, and a rural doctor's office or clinic would likely not be able to support our needs.

*There must be a hospital in the other direction,* I thought, hoping we wouldn't encounter unmaintained bumpy roads similar to those we'd traveled on yesterday.

"How long before we get there? We need to get there immediately—how long?" I asked the only person standing, not initially realizing he probably had little idea what I was saying in my panicked voice. I pointed to my left wrist where my watch would normally be and raised my arm.

"One hour," was his response in Spanish after a short discussion with the driver.

"One hour?" Jenn exclaimed back in English, making sure I knew what he'd said.

"That's not acceptable. We need to get there before that," I said. I looked at Jenn and then back at the park ranger, but before I could say any more, I felt a slight tug on my shirt from Julie. Jenn and Ludovic were speaking to each other in Spanish, and they began a dialogue with the park ranger in his native tongue. Julie gave me a nod and a small smile. It was difficult to be patient, but maybe additional speed wasn't the answer we needed. They assured us we would arrive at the hospital as soon as possible. For the time being, I stopped asking about arrival times and focused on CPR.

"Do you know what might have happened to her?" I asked, looking first at Julie and then at Ludovic.

Ludovic opened his mouth, then paused. "We cannot know for sure what happened. Does she have any medical conditions?"

"No," I said, shaking my head. "None that I'm aware of."

"It could be any number of things. Her heart, an aneurism . . . I would only be speculating," Ludovic continued. I sensed that he wanted to provide an answer to my question but didn't want to say too much.

Ludovic provided most of the chest compressions while Julie and I delivered the rescue breaths. Though he never said he was getting tired, I could see a strain on Ludovic's face. Providing constant CPR, particularly on a soft stretcher, was not easy work. I gave him a nod, indicating we should switch positions, but he shook his head. After a short while, it seemed clear he was tiring, and as I started to move past Julie, he again shook his head suggesting he could continue. Only after I moved my hands over his did he stop and allow me to take over.

The road was smoother than expected, though full of many sharp curves. We lost our balance several times as the unsympathetic laws of motion easily thrust our bodies one way and then another. Occasional potholes and bumps in the road made mouth-to-mouth breathing particularly challenging to administer.

Just as Julie moved her mouth toward Val, we hit a significant pothole. The downward movement met the sudden bounce upward, and the instantaneous collision propelled Julie's head backward. The damage was done. Julie grabbed her mouth, and blood began dripping from her lip.

I felt horrible about Julie's injury, and not wanting to cause her any further harm, I slid across the seat to take over the breaths. Other thoughts now entered my mind for the first time. Julie and Ludovic had never hesitated in helping Valerie, including direct mouth-to-mouth resuscitation. As trained professionals, they would know the risks this type of assistance would entail. The potential existed for Valerie's ailment to be contagious, and any number of blood-borne diseases would always be a possibility. Maybe this was a fear for them, but they never showed it—it did not interfere with their sense of duty, or mere kindness, to save a life. The opposite was also true, as any repercussions of a stranger's blood dripping into Val's mouth didn't worry me.

Valerie's condition hadn't improved. The signs of recovery that we believed we'd seen in the room were no longer there. The expelling of air had ceased, and now a small trickle of white-silvery fluid mixed with red blood leaked from Val's mouth.

The weight of helplessness was agonizing. As feelings of desperation swirled around in my head, I tried to rationalize that everything would be okay. We were likely getting close to an emergency room, with advanced medicine and equipment. That was the good part. I believed Valerie was somehow fighting for her life though unable to move or speak. Maybe her body was in some sort of comatose state that was helping her survive until we could get additional help. Even with my jumbled thoughts, I had a sense of determination, my heightened level of anxiety, fear and worry focused toward Valerie's recovery. She would make it. We—I—would see to that.

My mind moved from "what if" to "what happened?" *It makes no sense to me—how could this have happened?* I kept mulling over and over what was wrong and what possibly could have caused her condition.

Jenn was sitting closest to the back of the ambulance, gently rubbing Valerie's feet and saying words of encouragement.

*Valerie would really appreciate that.* She always loved it when someone rubbed her feet. I smiled appreciatively at Jenn but was completely oblivious to what Jenn was thinking at the time.

As Jenn rubbed Valerie's feet, fears she'd expressed in my room at Tikal now occupied a permanent space in her head. She looked for signs of a bite, a sting, or any marks from an animal, for, in her mind, that most certainly must have caused Val's condition. Looking at Valerie had become particularly difficult for Jenn, and extreme guilt overwhelmed her. She had convinced herself that their decision over who got which room might have killed her friend. She dwelled on the conversation she and Valerie had about our children and how they were so important to her, and she questioned how she could live with herself for putting her friend in this position.

"I did this to her," Jenn said under her breath. "It should be me lying there." She felt a foreboding feeling move through her body and enter her very soul.

My eyes moved from Jenn, along Valerie's body, and to her hands—in particular, the ends of her fingers. A grayish-blue discoloration spread across her fingernails and the surrounding skin from their tips to almost the first knuckle. I looked back at the foot in Jenn's hands, and it too appeared slightly discolored, more pronounced at the ends of Val's toes. I turned away and could not look again. This abrupt discovery was alarming. Val might be in worse shape than I had thought.

"Please tell the driver to hurry," I said, looking at Ludovic, then turning back to the park assistant, who was now seated next to the driver.

"Are we close to the hospital?" I asked.

"*Cinco minutos más,*" said the park ranger, the same answer of "five more minutes" he'd given us ten minutes earlier.

"Have you called them?" I asked, looking at what appeared to be a phone on his belt. "Please call the hospital and tell them we are on our way. They need to be ready for us when we get there." No movement or words came from the front of the vehicle.

Urging the driver to push the ambulance harder was doing no good. Valerie required equipment, medicine, and a medical team, but all we could do was use our own hands to keep her alive and wait to arrive at some distant hospital.

For the first time, an alternative outcome crossed my mind, and I tried to push the strange thoughts from my mind. The realization that Valerie's life might end here in this remote part of the world was horrifying. I pleaded with Valerie not to die.

"Valerie, we're almost there. Hang in there, Val. You need to make it. Valerie, don't you die. Oh, God, please don't let Valerie die."

# Chapter 10

## Santa Elena / Flores, Peten

Even from my limited vantage point, I could tell we'd reached a more populated area, though the first structures we passed appeared meager and in various levels of disrepair. I had no idea how large the town was, though it seemed large enough to support a commercial business base, in which case a hospital would certainly be part of its infrastructure. We'd made the trip to the edge of civilization in less time than our driver's initial estimate of one hour.

"I think we're close," Jenn said to the group. Julie looked up and provided a slight nod.

In an area indistinguishable from the residential neighborhoods we'd just passed, the ambulance suddenly stopped. I could see a larger building in the distance but no hospital name and only some dim lighting on the inside. *We made it,* I thought, not really concerning myself with how the outside looked.

We continued CPR but tried to study our new surroundings. I looked out the front window again and this time noticed a formidable metal gate preventing us from proceeding farther.

"You should have called ahead," were the first words out of my mouth. "I asked you to call. We should have . . ."

The truck's horn pierced the otherwise still night air, and my remaining words were lost. The driver clenched his teeth as he pushed hard on the center of the steering wheel and stared at the obstacle in front of him. I heard the ambulance's rear door open and glanced to my left just in time to see Jenn exit and close the door in one motion. Ludovic, Julie and I continued CPR without missing a compression. How could we arrive at the hospital and not get in? My mind tried to comprehend how something so unbelievable could happen.

After the next two rescue breaths, I looked out the window and saw someone scaling the gates just in front of the truck. "Is that Jenn?" A nod from Julie confirmed the person climbing the gate was indeed Jennifer. With assistance from the park ranger, Jenn climbed to the top of the gate, made it over, and disappeared out of sight.

Jenn ran to what she assumed was the front entrance, grabbed the handles of the glass doors, and started shaking them and screaming. The building, as well as the surrounding area, was dark, but she had traveled a long way and had no intention of being denied entry.

The combination of flashing lights, sirens, pounding fists, and yelling eventually reached a person inside, and a single light turned on inside the doorway. The woman under the light didn't look particularly interested in helping anyone, much less opening the door to someone wildly beating on glass and yelling in the middle of the night. Jenn continued to express her desire to enter, and it seemed the woman inside wanted only for the commotion to stop, but eventually realized Jenn wouldn't simply go away. She motioned Jenn to go around the building to the back, and from the look on her face, she didn't intend to open the front door.

Turning away from the door, Jenn quickly realized she had another problem. She could neither get in the building—as the person inside had already left and turned off the light—nor could she reach the ambulance without climbing over the iron gates. The boost from the park ranger that had propelled her over the gate was not available on this side of the fence. Without time to dwell on complex alternatives, Jenn noticed a metal-legged chair to her left and positioned it in front of the gate. She moved back and ran at the chair. One foot on the chair and the other on the first crossbeam of the gate, Jenn miraculously hoisted herself up and over the iron barricade.

Jenn directed the ambulance driver to move parallel to the hospital and down a small street. *How could the ambulance driver not know where the emergency entrance is located?* I thought. We made a quick left turn into an alleyway, and the ambulance stopped again.

This time we all exited, and a sense of renewed hope washed over me. We were only seconds away from getting to the emergency room and securing the help Valerie needed. Though we had no idea of the name of the facility or even the town we were in, considering where we'd come from, I was thankful to be at the hospital.

The back entrance to the hospital was different from what I'd expected. No iron gates here, but no large doors either— only a single door opening in the side of a cinder-block building that contained no actual door. The open entrance seemed more like a delivery passageway to a warehouse than a hospital entrance. *Maybe this is a shortcut to the emergency room*, I reasoned.

I didn't initially notice that no doctors or medical staff greeted us and no gurneys with medical bags were prepared for our arrival. As I focused on the new surroundings, a person who appeared to be a custodian motioned us to an open area and then to our right into a semi-enclosed room.

"Is this the right place?" I said as I looked at the dirty fabric curtain he'd just slid along its worn metal support rod. The room consisted of two painted cinder-block walls jutting out from the taller outside wall. The interior walls were approximately seven feet high and completely open at the top. The interior back wall was like the exterior wall, built of roughly eight-by-sixteen-inch blocks. The three-sided room held nothing on its walls and accommodated only a few notable items. In the center was a tall, narrow metal table with spindly legs. A cloth draped over its top hung off the table at both ends. A tall lamp with a flexible top section and a standard incandescent lightbulb sat in the corner of the room. Just outside the room, past the sliding curtain, was an open area lined with two dated desks, reminiscent of aged school desks you would find in the basement of a geology department.

The room's appearance was completely underwhelming but I hoped not completely inadequate for Valerie's needs.

This wasn't a high-tech medical facility, and it reinforced the fact that we were indeed in a remote part of the world. My optimism upon reaching a hospital wavered; however, fine ambiance wasn't what we were after. As long as we had access to medicine and equipment, regardless of the appearance or a calming atmosphere, Val would make it.

We positioned the stretcher next to the metal table and tried to raise it to table height, but the stretcher wouldn't budge from its lowest position. The hospital's doctors hadn't made it to our room yet, so we lifted Valerie's body awkwardly to the elevated table. She was now ready to receive all the benefits a hospital could supply.

There had been no change in Valerie's condition, and we restarted CPR. I noticed only two other people in the hospital: the person I'd initially thought was the custodian, who now appeared to be the resident medical expert, and a woman, the one whom I presumed had turned on the light and motioned us toward the back of the hospital. Their wide-eyed reactions to our situation provided insight into their experience level and medical training. The male hospital attendant looked at Val, walked around her body, and tried to smell her breath.

My enthusiasm continued to wane, and desperation came flooding back. The highly anticipated hospital—one with all the life-saving amenities—was not where we currently found ourselves.

Under normal circumstances, I might have intuitively known that a small-town hospital in northern Guatemala would have limited offerings. That realization was becoming clear and hor-rifying to think about, so I tried to restrain any discouraging thoughts.

*Maybe the resident doctors are still on their way. Maybe the medical equipment is just in another room,* I thought, reminding myself to stay positive.

We were trying to administer CPR, but on the elevated table the procedure was even more difficult. Ludovic was speaking with the male hospital attendant in Spanish, and it appeared he was once again taking control of the situation.

We didn't spend time speculating on the cause of Valerie's condition, nor did we chitchat about possible outcomes. This was our final destination. There was nowhere else to go, and we would need to make our stand to save Valerie's life here and now.

Though I did not understand Ludovic's orders, Julie, Jenn and the hospital staff moved quickly on separate missions to procure supplies. No scrubbing of hands or ripping open sterile bags full of new equipment, no iodine or alcohol wipes—just what was carried back from the supply room was what we began with. The items included a long, skinny, slightly curved metal device; a well-used electric pump mounted on a wheeled cart; and a piece of clear plastic tubing, one end of which was attached to the pump. The pump looked similar to one I'd seen in my father's shed as a child.

I didn't see Ludovic and Julie exchange gestures showing their aggravation, maybe because I chose not to see them, but Jenn would later tell me they'd indeed traded more than one exasperated look. The dearth of appropriate supplies and meager facilities was exponentially frustrating, but giving up because of these inadequacies was not an option.

It didn't take a medical genius to determine the intent of the items brought into the room. Though I didn't know the words *tracheal intubation,* I guessed we were about to place the tube through Val's mouth and somehow into her airway.

Ludovic maneuvered the elongated metal object past Valerie's teeth and into her throat, then tried to guide the tubing along the metal device into position. It wasn't working. In an effort to get a better angle, Ludovic jumped onto the narrow table, straddling his knees on the sides of Val's body. Finally the tube advanced along the metal object and out of sight into Valerie's body.

Success was not long-lived. When Ludovic left the room, presumably in search of other lifesaving items, the tube came out of Valerie's mouth. Julie grabbed it from the floor and started the process again. I thought I could tell how it worked, but we weren't succeeding. I moved around the back of Val's head and raised her chin, thinking it might help with the insertion. Julie did not tell me to stop.

"Aw!" Julie said, more a sound of frustration than an actual word. She wasn't happy with our unsuccessful attempts to reinsert the breathing tube.

"Here, let me take this thing and you take the tube," I said to Julie, thinking we needed to change strategies. Trying to be as gentle as possible in positioning the device into Valerie's somewhat stiffened jaw was neither easy nor pleasant.

"*En*," said Julie. I wasn't sure if that was French for "in" or just an unintelligible noise, but the air of triumph in her voice suggested it was a small success.

With one end of the plastic tube in Val's body and the other attached to the small black pump, we turned the switch on. The sound of the aged machinery was yet another harsh reality. The apparatus attached to Val looked horrible. After another disconnection, we slid the table toward the corner of the room, hoping a few more inches of space would make the difference. Either the electric cord to the pump was too short or the tubing wasn't long enough, or both, but the tubing detached from the pump or came out of Valerie's mouth several times.

It did flash though my mind that the tubing, now placed well into Valerie's body, had likely not been sterile to begin with, and after falling to the floor twice, it certainly wasn't. The thought of bacteria and who knows what other debris entering Val's system wasn't even close to our major concern.

As they were looking for other supplies, Ludovic and Jenn found a slightly longer tube, and the process started again. Eventually all components were working as intended, though, as we stepped back, it provided little comfort. The little puffing sounds from the electric pump and the opaque plastic tube going into Valerie's mouth did not seem like the life-saving solution we needed.

Julie and Ludovic continued discussions with the hospital attendants in Spanish but gained little useful information, and the staff's initial interest had diminished. It now appeared the hospital staff wanted little to do with what had so rudely interrupted their night's shift. With reluctance, the male employee went to a small room along the far side of the commons area and returned with a vial of clear liquid and a syringe with a needle already attached. The sight gave me pause, as I imagined the needle was, at best, not sterile and, at worst, had been used previously. The thought instantaneously departed as Ludovic swiftly inserted the serum into Valerie's right forearm.

The hospital and its amenities were far below our expectations and certainly below our needs. The location was better than where we'd started a few hours ago but not all that much better. A larger hospital—and air transport—would likely be necessary.

I remembered that not everyone traveling to Tikal opted for the more remote route we had relied on yesterday. Tourists had an option of flying to a place near Tikal, and maybe there was an airport near our current location.

"Jenn, we need a helicopter or plane. Maybe they have some life-flight medical service we could use," I suggested naively.

Jenn already knew we needed another hospital and transportation, as she'd discussed the subject with Julie.

Julie typically spoke to Jenn in Spanish, as English was Julie's third language. Jenn didn't understand every word of their conversations, but it was clear from Julie's voice that Valerie needed additional medical assistance to save her life.

Valerie's condition appeared to be unchanged to me, though thoughts of quitting our efforts never crossed my mind. Julie and Ludovic continued to attend to Val with unrelenting determination.

"You're going to make it, Val. Just hold on," I said repeatedly.

When Julie approached Jenn a second time, Jenn was already shaking her head.

"I knew we weren't in a good place when we walked in," Jenn said to Julie. "Did you see this?" Jenn said, pointing to bloody finger marks on the wall just around the corner from where they were standing.

"We need a larger hospital with additional supplies and equipment. This isn't going to work," Julie said.

Jenn, once again on a mission, started talking to the hospital staff and the ambulance drivers about hospital and transportation options. Their conversation suggested there was indeed an airport in town, and it seemed like the best place to start.

# Chapter 11

## Planes, Dogs, Military and Money

The park rangers were more than willing to take Jenn to the airport to see if she could arrange for an emergency evacuation. Her ride to the airport was quick during the early-morning hours, and the flashing lights and siren made sure no one crossed their path. Not until the vehicle stopped did Jenn learn the military was in charge of the closed and guarded airport. Jenn needed to first arrange special admission via the military officer stationed at the main entrance. After some negotiations, Jenn and the two park rangers were making their way through the airport compound. Most buildings were dark and showed no signs of activity. Their destination, as relayed to them by the guard, was a single-level office complex located at one end of the airport. They arrived at what they thought was the correct building; at least it was a place to start.

Even with the brilliant lights and noise of the ambulance, it still took a pounding fist on the door to get the attention of the Santa Elena/Flores airport staff. Once inside, Jenn and the park rangers tried to explain the situation and its urgency to the military personnel. English wasn't spoken, so Jenn did her best to communicate, though the Spanish discussion was difficult.

Over time, Jenn learned the airport contained no planes that could support our needs, or at least ones they would allow us to use for such a purpose. They did suggest that suitable transport might exist in Guatemala City.

One of the men in his military fatigues picked up the telephone and started to dial.

"Progress," Jenn said under her breath.

Jenn listened to one side of the telephone conversation, keenly aware that time was slipping away. She soon became impatient with the discussion that seemed to be going in circles.

"Is there a plane or not?" Jenn asked after waiting as long as she could. "If so, when can we get it here?" These questions seemed relatively simple to answer.

"We will let you talk," said one of the men to Jenn as he dialed another number. Jenn prepared herself to convince whomever was on the other end of the line. The person who answered the phone sounded much different than she'd expected. Then again, everything was different than she'd expected. Jenn quickly told the person what had happened and what she needed. "We are in an emergency situation and have absolutely no time to spare."

"Jenn, Jennifer . . . is this Jennifer? This is Julie," said the other person on the call.

"Julie? What—why am I talking to you?" replied Jenn, speaking both into the phone and to the men in the room.

"I don't know. The phone just kept ringing. It's the phone on the desk outside of the room here. No one was answering it, so I did," said Julie.

"But I thought . . . They told me I would be speaking with someone at the Guatemala City airport," said Jenn, again speaking so others in the room could hear.

"Jenn, make sure they know it must be a special medical airplane; a regular plane will not work," Julie added.

"What are you talking about?"

"Medical supplies. We can't take them on a regular plane and . . ." Her words switched to a string of French that Jenn didn't understand, though she understood the gist of Julie's remarks. The specific type of airplane seemed far too detailed, as Jenn was willing to take any form of transport.

From additional discussions with the men at the airport, the question now appeared to have come down to one thing—one thousand US dollars, to be exact. Though they didn't explicitly tell Jenn a plane was available, Jenn got the feeling someone's private plane in Guatemala City might be available for the right amount of money. Jenn knew she could raise the money and desperately tried to tell them this. "No, I don't have the money on me now," she said, pointing at her body, suggesting there was no place to put the money.

Jenn was dressed only in a small nightshirt, a light cover shawl she'd grabbed just prior to leaving the bungalow in Tikal, and lacey white sleeping shorts—acutely aware of her minimalistic outfit.

They were at an impasse. There were no airplanes or helicopters available for flight out of Santa Elena, but with the right amount of cash, one might become available from another city. She decided to get back to the hospital and relay the news. Jenn thanked everyone and walked outside, shutting the door behind her.

The drivers were waiting for Jenn to finish and were already in the ambulance. She walked toward the vehicle and caught movement of two dogs near the far end of the building. Jenn hadn't seen any dogs before, and no one mentioned anything about watchdogs on the grounds. As Jenn approached the ambulance, forty yards or so away, the dogs continued their advance. Her pulse quickened as the faster she walked, the faster they approached. The drivers, witnessing the standoff, opened the ambulance door and waved at her to hurry up, but they remained in the vehicle. Jenn's eyes darted from the waiting vehicle to the dogs and back to the vehicle, and she knew they had no intention of putting themselves between her and the dogs.

The rangers yelled out the window at Jenn to get into the truck. At a full sprint, she reached the vehicle and closed the door behind her. Jenn was winded and angry, but she was otherwise safe. Running from guard dogs hadn't been on the agenda, but then again, nothing had been. She took several deep breaths, wanting to scream, but she only sighed. Soon the noise of the barking dogs, and her pounding heart, were drowned out by the sound of ambulance sirens.

We never closed the curtain in front of Val's room, as someone was constantly moving in and out. We'd worked so hard to get the pump and its appendages to work, even chipping Valerie's tooth during the process, but the tubing came out of Valerie's throat yet again, and we abandoned our efforts to reinsert it. I continued chest compressions, and Julie administered artificial breathing by squeezing a breathing bag we had found in one of the supply closets.

Another clear liquid, which I assumed was a type of adrenaline—though I didn't know for sure—was injected into Val's forearm. The medicine again appeared to have no effect on Valerie's condition.

The enthusiasm of reaching the hospital was over, as was the flurry of trying new equipment and finding medicine for Val. We were back to the same thing I'd started on the floor of a small jungle room more than two hours ago. I was numb with despair and disorientation.

"Do you have any children?" asked Julie.

It took me a while to absorb the question, as it seemed odd to be thinking about other things besides Val's condition.

"Uh, yeah. Three."

It seemed as if the world had stopped. Everything I'd done over the past couple of hours had focused on one thing. Her question suggested the earth was still revolving, and other things were still happening. Maybe not everything had stopped. Thousands of miles away, three children lay tucked in their beds sleeping soundly, looking forward to a Saturday and having fun with Grandma and Grandpa. Each blissfully unaware we were desperately fighting to save their mother's life.

"How old are they?" Julie inquired.

Again, thinking about such things was difficult for me.

"What? Uh . . . thirteen, eleven . . . uh . . . let's see . . . eight." Thoughts of my children and possible dramatic changes in their lives flooded into my mind. Consequences for my children were painfully difficult to comprehend. *What if the kids never see their mother alive again? What? No, no. That's not an option. I'm not going to let that happen. I can't think about that. I'm not ready for this.* I closed my eyes in an effort to clear my mind of such nonsense.

"All we need is a flight to a real hospital," I said to Julie, changing the subject.

I heard the ambulance returning from the airport, and almost immediately, Jenn was in the room.

"We located the airport. There's no plane there. We made some calls and talked with several people. It may cost some money, but there are private planes that might work," Jenn explained.

Spending money was also something I hadn't considered, and I was ready to empty any bank account or borrow any amount necessary.

Jenn seemed pleased about the possible breakthrough in finding a plane, which buoyed my spirits.

"Great work, Jenn. When can we go?" I responded with hope in my voice.

"They're not ready yet but could be relatively soon," said Jenn.

Julie nodded in agreement. Ludovic was in another room, probably looking for additional supplies.

As we would soon discover, not everything we were told would turn out to be true or even possible.

The telephone, conveniently located on the desk opposite Val's space, came in handy as we shifted between tasks. Jenn and I spoke with several people regarding our medical transportation needs, and we established that their main concern was if I was willing to and could afford to pay for their services. They explained it would cost a thousand dollars to charter the plane that, even back then, seemed like a bargain. They also wanted to know when we would be ready to leave and specifically where we would like to go. This of course raised other concerns in our minds. If these people were involved in the medical transportation business, they should know the best place to take a patient. Looking back, the assumption that these people had anything to do with medical transportation was a ridiculous notion.

In subsequent calls, they stated they would need to construct a flight plan, file it with government authorities, and fuel the plane. They could possibly be ready in a few hours. To someone calmly making a standard flight reservation, these items and their timing would be valid. To me, their timetable was illogical bordering on insane.

My wife lay dying fifteen feet from the very spot where I now stood. I was going back and forth from phone calls to CPR to asking Julie and Ludovic what else we could do. The people on the phone, whom I barely understood, clearly did not understand our situation or me.

"Where would you like to travel?" came another voice on the other end of the telephone line.

"Where would I like to travel?" *Are you kidding me? We've discussed this ten times. What do you not understand? We need the fastest way possible to a get to a large and at least somewhat competent hospital.* I was on the verge of completely losing it, but knowing this might be our only hope out of there, I kept my thoughts to myself.

"Yes, yes, I will pay. No, I don't have the cash on me, but I will give you my credit card information or I'll get the money somehow." The circular conversations seemed much harder than they needed to be. The unbearable distraction of dealing with such stuff seemed senseless and removed valuable time with Valerie.

"Jenn, can you talk with this guy? Tell him we will do anything he wants if he can get us to where we need to go," I asked her.

"Why don't you go to the other hospital?" said the person I once thought was the janitor, who had now turned resident medical expert.

"What other hospital? There's another hospital? Are you kidding—another hospital?" I said, shaking my head. I moved to where Jenn was on the phone. "Jenn, there's another hospital. Let's forget about this guy you are talking to."

With the option of immediate air transportation becoming improbable, the possibility of another hospital gave me a glimmer of hope—even though the thought of going to the wrong hospital turned my stomach.

*How could we have gone to the wrong hospital? Had we been wasting time here?*

Jenn hung up the phone and switched her conversation to the person standing next to her. We needed to find out more about this hospital. Was it bigger or better? Did it have actual equipment and doctors? Was the hospital near our current location? With the new information and our ever-growing list of questions, Jenn was again moving. I went back to assist Ludovic and Julie with Val's blood flow and breathing.

# Chapter 12

## *Refuting the Unfathomable*

---

Some time had passed before I heard the word "Rod" from the familiar French voice. Ludovic touched my arm, motioning for me to stop CPR. As sincere as the gesture was, it was met with determined resistance. I was not giving up and neither should he.

"We need more time," I said, shaking my head from side to side. I continued chest compressions, but my eyes looked at Ludovic, hoping to convey my inner thoughts without words. *There must be more we can do. Someone else will be here soon to help. Jenn will find the other hospital. She will bring back the help we need, or we'll go there.*

Ludovic and Julie seemed to understand. They responded to my emotional request without hesitancy or additional comment.

CPR continued, though soon I began to feel the heavy weight of my arms and the tiredness of my own body. I was starting to see things with a slightly different perspective than just moments ago.

New questions came to my mind. *Are our efforts working? Are we providing the necessary sustenance to keep Val alive? Has she shown any improvements or changed at all since we arrived here?*

As I continued to compress Valerie's chest, for the second time that day, my eyes moved slowly down her long, slender body. I stopped my gaze at her feet, looking specifically at the ends of her toes. Then I looked at her hands. In both cases, the once-vibrant pink skin tone was gone. It seemed clear that her blood hadn't reached these extremities for quite some time.

My eyes moved from Val to Julie to Ludovic and then to the blank block wall on the other side of Valerie. My arms remained in their locked position, set for the next downstroke, but the movement did not occur. Poised for the next compression, I continued to stare at the painted block wall. I could push again at any time, but I did not. I had stopped.

I stood over Valerie, arms stretched over her chest, sensing Ludovic and Julie contemplating my next move, knowing they were allowing me to make the call. I gazed back at Valerie and realized her condition had not changed for a long time. I lifted my arms from atop her body and lowered them to my sides.

"Let me show you something," Ludovic said to me as he folded a tissue into quarter sections. He motioned me toward Val's head, and we bent down close to her face. He blotted the corner of the tissue on the exposed white of Val's eye. He showed me the tissue, then explained there was no longer any liquid surrounding her eye; it was dry. He then handed the tissue to me and gestured. He wanted me to check for myself. I did not doubt his ability as a doctor; I knew he was right. Nevertheless, I bent down close to Valerie's face and placed part of the folded tissue to the white part of Val's eye. It felt rigid and inflexible. There was no moisture, and it did not move.

Ludovic slowly shook his head and said, "She has expired."

I heard his words and moved from my bent position. I stood over Val's left shoulder, looking down at her. I did not cry—not then—or scream or become hysterical. I just looked upon her and wondered. There was no shock, disbelief, or denial. Those emotions, and many more, would fill me soon enough. In this moment, I just stood there seeing Valerie's body lying on the metal table, looking at her pretty face and long blond hair. She looked the same as the day we'd married.

My thoughts were clear and my mind open. *We couldn't save her.*

I broke my gaze from Val and looked at Ludovic and Julie. I looked back at Val and heard the curtain closing on the metal rod behind me. My mind was starting to engage once again, and other thoughts began to enter.

*No, this is not true. I thought we would save her. This did not happen. It can't happen.* I stared at Val and began to fill with anxiety, feeling a sudden weakness surrounding me, enveloping my very core. *She couldn't die. Val can't be dead. Oh my God—Valerie's dead.*

The clock on the wall above the small desk directly outside Val's cube said 6:20 a.m. Some of the documents would state the time of death at 5:00 a.m. and others would list 5:50 a.m. Maybe the last hour or so of working on Valerie had only been for my sake and no one had wanted to tell me, or maybe I'd just read the clock wrong. How could everything have happened so fast?

A scream broke the hospital's silence. Jenn had just discovered the news, and she was in disbelief. I could see Jenn looking though the partly opened curtain and not wanting to accept what she had just heard and was now seeing. Jenn's body went limp, her legs unable to hold her body steady. Ludovic was the closest and grabbed her as she went down. Julie was near her other side, and I ran to help Jenn to the floor. I held her head as Ludovic and Julie elevated her legs.

"Jenn, are you okay? I can't do this without you. Jenn, I need you. Can someone get some bottled water? Jenn—I can't lose you too," I said in a panicked voice. Jenn would not be the last person I would witness collapsing upon hearing the news of Val's death.

# PART III

*Unfamiliar People, Familiar Confusion*

# Chapter 13

## Checking the Clock

After a few minutes on the floor, Jenn recovered and was back on her feet. To regain the physical ability to stand was one thing. To regain the emotional understanding of the situation was quite another.

I went back into the room with Valerie and stared at her body in utter disbelief. Val had been alive, talking, eating, and laughing just a few short hours ago. How could she not have survived? The realization was staggering and much too hard to fully comprehend as everything in me rejected the premise and its conclusion. I looked at my wife and started to cry.

I pulled a small metal chair next to the table where Val lay, slid the cloth screen nearly closed, and sat down. *What now?* I thought. This was not a *what now* in terms of my life, family, work or an existence without her. Those things were to consider in the future. No, what I needed now was to get Valerie home.

We had made our travel plans only a month before, and the information was still relatively fresh in my mind. If I could get things to come together, there was a workable plan to get home today. I tried to remember our flight options. *I believe there's a flight out of Belize in the morning. Is it nine thirty . . . ten or eleven? Something like that. We need to be on that plane.*

What had happened right in front of my eyes seemed far from real. Emotions flooded my mind. I was in shock, yes, but it seemed like so much more. Feelings of anguish surrounded me, and then fear would take hold, then resentment. Each emotion fought for space in my mind. I tried to process what my mind would not accept—the fact that Valerie had died.

By moving my head slightly, I could still see the large clock above the desks through the opening in the curtain. I again wished I had found my wristwatch in the bungalow. As I stared at the wall clock, I made plans.

I was planning, thinking, and looking. We needed to consider options for the best way to return home, but in front of me was Valerie. She was there with me, and she looked as if she were sleeping.

The brief moment of planning was gone. I started to cry again. I had no need to be outwardly brave or show others I was strong, but when the emotions began rising up inside me, I tried to subdue them. I wanted to lie down on the floor, but I believed I might not get back up, and there were things that required my immediate attention. I snapped back from my deeply despondent thoughts and started thinking about logistics, such as moving Val's lifeless body and airline departure schedules. As I thought about these plans, here with me in this small room was Val, my wife, motionless on a narrow metal table. Two juxtaposed realities continued in my mind.

It was a little after six thirty, and if we left now, we could make a flight back to the States. Given the road conditions—at least the ones we'd encountered traveling here—it would be close. If we couldn't make the morning flight, maybe there was a flight later in the afternoon. I really did not want to wait that long, but if we had to take a later flight, that would still work. *Maybe we can use the private plane Jenn found. If we use that plane and leave immediately, I'm sure we can make the earlier flight.*

Of course, now this all seems absurd and irrational. Removing a dead body from a hospital, transporting it across two countries, and then onto an airplane for a flight to the United States obviously makes little sense. Nevertheless, I had a deep yearning to get back home with Val as soon as possible, regardless of how irrational. My mind began to cloud.

I sat on the small chair looking at Valerie, then the clock, then back to Val's body, making plans and formulating various exit strategies. I knew there would be some paperwork involved in order to move her body from the hospital and assumed that the hospital personnel were already preparing the necessary documents.

With the curtain closed, shutting out the rest of the world was consoling. In many ways, I wanted to stay behind the barrier, hoping my new and unfamiliar life would change or somehow just go away. Down deep, I knew it wouldn't. I didn't feel anger or resentment or try to place blame on any particular decision, place or person. Some of these feelings would hit me hard in the future, but they were not part of my thoughts as I sat alone with Valerie's body.

*How do I tell my kids, others? How could this have happened? What caused this?* None of us knew the answers to my questions. We needed to develop and implement a strategy that would get us out of the hospital and, eventually, home. With these thoughts in my mind, I stood and opened the curtain.

"Jenn? Where's Jennifer?" I asked, pushing the curtain aside. "We need to get out of this place. We need to get Val home as soon as possible." Jenn had been considering next steps as well and understood the urgency to arrange a strategy.

On the other side of the curtain, the room felt different than it had earlier in the morning. There were several more people standing in the common area. They were talking with one another in Spanish, and most of them I had never seen before. I presumed they were supplementary hospital staff, but in retrospect, I'm not sure. Jenn started a conversation with one of the male hospital assistants whom we'd seen from the beginning. Immediately there was a small crowd of people surrounding them. Ludovic and Julie quickly joined in the discussion.

Though I could not truly know what Jenn, Julie and Ludovic were thinking, their faces were telling and showed emotional strain, deep sorrow and defeat. Valerie's death was taking a toll on them as well.

Frustrated with not being able to understand the details of their discussions, I moved back into the small room and looked at Val. Just as the space outside the curtain had changed, so too was there a sense of change inside the room. The room was becoming lighter. Along the back wall of the room, three-quarters of the way up the wall, there was an opening. Not a glass-covered window opening but simply an open hole in the wall. In fact, as I looked to my left, I saw several of these openings along the back wall, each similar in size, approximately three feet long and eight inches high, with no barrier to the outside elements. The opening was good for natural light to enter, along with animals, insects or any unwelcome organisms.

"I can't believe those are just open like that," I said, shaking my head. The astonishment of this discovery did not last long, as it didn't take long before I was again thinking about departure options and how we could get home. I had no idea that, on the other side of the curtain, a series of events was unfolding in stark contrast with my expectations.

"We need an official to sign off and certify the death," Jenn said, sticking her head around the curtain without entering the room. "Ludovic has been talking with the hospital staff, and they're not going to allow the body to be removed until the official gets here and gives us some papers."

"Is this official person a doctor or associated with the hospital? Can we just get the guy who was here last night to sign the papers? He was here the whole time. Let's find him, and we can be on our way." It made sense to me that someone, presumably a doctor, would need to sign off on a death certificate. The fact the paperwork hadn't already been completed was surprising.

"That's not the person we need, Rod. I'm not sure that was even a doctor last night," Jenn said as her eyes started to well up with tears.

"I'm not surprised by that," I said, shaking my head. "When will this 'official' be here?"

"I'll ask again, but I think he's on his way now."

"*Él está en camino ahora,*" said someone we thought was yet another hospital staffer. Jenn translated the comment as "he is on his way now," and we genuinely believed this meant someone, at this very moment, was physically on his way to the hospital to help us.

*How big could this town be?* I thought, after looking at the clock over the desk yet again. I'd assumed it would only take a few minutes for the official to get here if he was on his way. It would take a little time to complete the paperwork, but we'd be able to take off soon after that. We would be cutting it close to make it to the Belize airport in time, however. I expressed this to Jenn, and in the back of my mind, I was thinking that private plane might still be an option.

The details of how we would travel with Valerie's body were yet to be determined. I thought the hospital likely had some sort of insulated container system for such occasions, but until we had the appropriate paperwork, we would not know for sure.

Fifteen minutes went by, then twenty and then forty minutes. "Why isn't he here? Can we call him?" I asked anyone who would listen. "I thought he was on his way. We're losing time." No new answers were available other than, "Yes, he is undoubtedly on his way," usually accompanied by a nod of the head.

Not being in control or, for that matter, even fully understanding the situation was difficult. For most of us, it had already been a long day, and without the necessary papers, it seemed it would not end anytime soon.

A horrible grief weighed on my body and those of my companions. I wanted to go back to last night, back to my old life. My mind was easily drawn into "if only" scenarios:

if only we would have done this or if only we had not done that. An atrocious sorrow was just below the surface, inviting me to give in to its vastness. I tried to temper these feelings by thinking about getting Val's body out of the hospital and back home as soon as possible. Though sobbing and mourning were part of each minute, I needed to do more than just sit and cry.

Jenn, Julie, Ludovic and I were doing what we could to communicate with anyone who showed any interest in listening. Jeff was still in Tikal, and the hospital staff said they had no way of contacting him. We needed to wait and be patient, but that was a lot to ask.

*"Hemos escuchado del funcionario,"* were the words from one of the medical staff members as they approached the group of people gathered near the hallway. I wasn't sure what the comment meant, but they seemed excited to share the news.

"I think they heard from the official," Jenn told me in her best translation. We eventually discovered, though we were never completely sure, that the official we were waiting for was the equivalent of a coroner.

"It sounds like he was delayed due to another accident. They are saying he will arrive shortly."

*Yet another "shortly,"* I thought. This time I curbed my enthusiasm.

Time advanced, minute by minute, and our window of opportunity to get Val's body moved to another location slipped away with it.

The sound of a vehicle starting in the alleyway caught me by surprise. The noise grabbed Jenn's attention as well, and we moved outside through the same open doorway we had entered. The two park rangers were heading back to Tikal with the ambulance. To the extent it could, the ambulance had served its purpose. Julie and Ludovic were also outside sitting on a short block wall. Julie had her head on Ludovic's shoulder, and he had his arms around her. They looked defeated but united in their somber embrace.

"I wish Jeff was here with us," Jenn said. "He has no idea what has happened since the ambulance left his sight. He doesn't know that Valerie died. I'm not sure he even knows where we are."

"Thanks for coming with me, Jenn," I replied. "We'll get word to Jeff, and he'll find us." Though I wasn't sure how we would make that happen.

# Chapter 14

## *The Official*

Additional people found their way into the portion of the hospital we occupied and, with them, more confusion. The two staff members we'd dealt with in the middle of the night had been little help in saving Valerie's life, but their faces were familiar, and that alone provided a mysterious level of comfort to us. We couldn't say the same about all the new members of the staff circling around.

Disbelief of Valerie's death settled in, as did an ever-increasing anxiety and feelings of unfamiliarity and remoteness. At the height of our trying to save Val's life, little else had mattered, and other than the lack of support, equipment, and supplies, details of our surroundings had largely gone unnoticed. Now, as we waited for others to act, feelings of isolation grew. It became abundantly clear we were dealing with this perplexingly tragic event in a world very distant and different from the one we knew. We had no travel guides to reference, we could not pick up the telephone and call someone, and no one we knew would be lending a hand. With the language and cultural barriers, communication was difficult. Though some had second or third languages that matched those of others, understanding subtle points of a conversation wasn't easy. Jenn and I soon realized there was no single source of information, no one person to take our burden, to provide comfort, or to say, or even hint, that everything would be all right.

Having grown up an only child in rural Minnesota, I knew the basic concept of doing things on my own. Valerie would often comment about this aspect of my life, as my actions in certain situations were much different from her own instincts. I tended to hunker down and isolate, detach and think my way through a particular circumstance. Though I had never encountered anything like this, my instincts followed a predictable path. We needed to see a way through the obstacles ourselves.

The official coroner whom we had anxiously been waiting for finally arrived. He was slightly older than most of the people in the room, and his suit and tie distinguished him even more from the off-white clothes of the hospital staff. He did not speak to us directly, just looked at me and muttered a few brief words to one of the hospital staff members before moving to the body lying on the metal table a few feet from where we stood. He removed the thin sheet we had placed on top of Valerie, and he started to scan her body. He rotated his head as he quickly eyed her entire body, and then he touched her arms and legs. He moved close to her face, lightly sniffing the air around it. With one more rapid look around the room, he was done.

*Interesting,* I thought. I'd figured it would not take long for the coroner to complete his work, and this quick assessment meant that we would be on our way soon.

By the time the coroner completed his examination and exited the room, three additional people were waiting for him in the common area. Two of them were staring uncomfortably at me. The official approached the group of men and started talking.

The conversation was difficult to understand even for Jenn and Ludovic, who were reasonably fluent in the language, and impossible for me to understand.

"Where's he going?" Jenn said as the official turned and headed for the door.

"Hey, wait. Don't we get some paperwork . . . documents or something? Can we move her out now?" I called out.

The official stopped and turned to yet another person whom I'd never seen before. Jenn and Ludovic started talking to the group. They desperately tried to explain the situation and asked when we would get the signed papers we needed. As with many of the conversations, it became highly animated.

The discussion ended suddenly, and the official looked up. "I need to write this up, and then a doctor will need to see her before she can be released from the hospital," said the official in English. He turned around once again and left the room.

"What? Are they kidding? We were told all we needed was this guy's signature on some papers," I said to Jenn.

The official was gone, and we now had more questions than before. Our subsequent discussions with the hospital staff, and the other people who had appeared at the hospital, didn't provide satisfactory answers to most of them.

"I guess the official was simply here to make sure that Val—they call her the American woman—died in their hospital of natural causes and that no crime was committed," Jenn said.

"A crime! They think a crime was committed? Is that why the official and his friends were looking at me so strangely? They think I did something to Val? I suppose that's why there are so many people here, just in case they needed to arrest me."

"The official doesn't think a crime was committed. He could not smell any alcohol, and he did not see anything suspicious," Jenn said.

"Didn't smell alcohol. What does that mean?"

"I'm not completely sure. That's just what I thought he said. Let's leave it be for now."

As I listened to Jenn, I contemplated what I had just heard. *They're thinking I had something to do with Val's death.* To think of such a thing was extremely unsettling and bewildering, yet it made sense to me. *Why wouldn't they consider that possibility?* I thought, as my contempt began to diminish. They needed to consider that option, no matter how absurd the concept was to me. Then I wondered about a possible alternative finding. *What if the official hadn't made this ruling?* I'd never thought about a Guatemalan prison or how their criminal justice system might or might not work. Though I did think it would likely have significantly delayed our departure.

"An actual medical doctor will need to handle the death certificate," Jenn added.

"We're waiting for a doctor to sign off. We're at a hospital, for Christ's sake. There should be plenty of people here who can do that."

"I get the feeling it's not that easy, Rod. There may not be a doctor here who can complete it right now."

"There're no doctors here? Where the hell are they? What kind of hospital is this?" I said, disgust coming through with each word. The repulsed look on Jenn's face said she was as upset as I was. This clearly was disturbing news. By this point, bad news was becoming the norm. One step forward, two steps backward.

As frustrated as we all felt, our general demeanor remained relatively calm and even-keeled, considering the circumstances. But this wasn't the case with the Guatemalans. Their voices would go from standard volume to practically yelling at each other and then back down again in a single conversation. Several times I found myself wondering if they would come to blows before the conversation was over.

"Okay, if we need a doctor, let's find a doctor," I said. It seemed ridiculous but our only option.

"We will need to go to the other hospital. There must be a doctor there who can come over here and sign off," Jenn said.

"Why did those park rangers bring us here in the first place if there was another hospital? Maybe that hospital had real doctors and actual medical equipment. What is this place, anyway?" I said. For the third time that morning, we'd discussed another hospital. The very thought of a medical facility nearby that could have helped save Valerie's life turned my stomach.

I needed to clear my head and consider the consequences of the most recent events. I needed to see Val. I walked ten feet to my right, moved around the thin cloth drape, and entered the small room where Valerie's body was waiting. I had accomplished nothing since I'd left, and now I wondered if the other hospital offered more than a rigid metal table.

Seeing Valerie's body lying there triggered immediate sorrow, though I had no idea how vast this loss would eventually become. Even in her current state, my instincts drew me to her. There seemed to be something at work here that I could not put my finger on. When the outside events started to close in, here was where I came. The scene inside the room was far from tranquil, and it was maddening to see Valerie's lifeless body, but it did provide a strange and unmistakable feeling of solace being next to her. I do not have any explanations for why I felt this way; I just did.

Our situation was becoming more complex, and departing the hospital, traveling between countries, and making a morning flight, or any flight that day, seemed no longer possible. We needed to formulate another solution, a new escape plan. With this realization, much of my hope vanished, and a heaviness took its place.

"Rod, I would like you to meet someone," Jenn said, looking though the curtain's opening. Pulled out of my trancelike state, it took an extra few seconds to realize someone was talking to me.

"This is Edmundo," Jenn said, introducing me to someone I'd never seen before. "He's the son of the owner of the Jaguar Inn."

Edmundo was in his late twenties or early thirties with long, curly brown hair and a friendly face. I stood up from my chair and shook his hand.

"He said we could use the phones at the inn, and if we needed anything to just ask," Jenn continued. This seemed to be good news, though I didn't know exactly what it meant. His gesture was comforting, and knowing someone else was reaching out to help, someone who perhaps knew the system, was a positive step.

It turned out the Jaguar Inn had a sister hotel in Santa Elena/ Flores under similar management, and, as would happen in most places, the death of a hotel guest garnered the attention of the owner.

Word of an unusual event travels quickly—and rural Guatemala was no exception—particularly the death of an American woman.

Edmundo seemed sincere in his response, and his grasp of English was the best we'd encountered so far. We certainly could use transportation between Tikal and the hospital, and possibly from our current location and the other hospital if that was required. Edmundo stated we were welcome to use his minivan. Any effort to assist us was highly welcomed.

One of our first requests of him was to ask the hospital staff specifically about our options. We hoped the answer would be different this time. Edmundo did not hesitate and began a discussion with several hospital staffers. The replies suggested that going to another hospital or getting another doctor to help us would not be possible. We started to wonder if the hospital staff had any idea how to proceed or whom to contact next.

We took a step back and focused on what we knew. The official who'd examined Val had determined he would not pursue a criminal investigation and clearly stated we needed a doctor to sign papers. It looked as if we had no option but to follow his direction. So far, we had been unsuccessful in locating a doctor to complete the paperwork. Perhaps a consulate or embassy, if any was nearby, might be able to help. We'd been trying to solve our dilemma ourselves, but the further we went, the more complex it became, and if a governmental entity could help, we would let them. Edmundo knew of no such entities near here. However, there was a US Embassy in Guatemala City. We agreed we should give them a call.

"The hotel here in Santa Elena is the best place to do this," Edmundo said. "We can make telephone calls, and we have a two-way radio setup between Tikal and our hotel here. Cell phones do not work well in Tikal."

"I also need to contact Jeff. I'll go with Edmundo," Jenn said.

"Okay, ask Jeff if he can gather up our stuff from the room. I'm sure it's scattered everywhere," I said. I could only imagine what the small room looked like in the daylight with the contents of two backpacks strewn about and the beds turned on their sides. Though probably not physically taxing, I suspected the chore would be mentally uncomfortable for Jeff.

"Of course, he'll need to get our bags packed and be ready to go when Edmundo's minivan arrives. I think they're going to take Julie back to Tikal as well," said Jenn.

Julie knew there was no additional assistance she could provide here at the hospital. She and Ludovic had several travel companions back at Tikal, and she could provide them an update on the situation and let them know she and Ludovic were okay. Ludovic decided to stay with us. Though we encouraged him to go along with Julie, his decision to stay was comforting.

Jenn and Edmundo headed out toward Edmundo's vehicle to make their way to the Santa Elena Jaguar Inn.

Needing to consider what additional steps might be necessary and how our newest plan altered the previous one, I instinctively walked back into the now-familiar room, pulled the curtain three-quarters of the way shut, and sat down on the chair next to Val. A new getting-home-strategy was in motion, though looking at Valerie's body, the progress felt hollow. The situation was becoming overwhelming.

"What else can I do?" Edmundo asked Jenn once they reached the van.

Not really knowing what to say, Jenn asked, "Can you locate a priest?"

# Chapter 15

## *Waiting to Hear*

---

J enn was nervous and anxious, as an official-sounding male voice on the other end of the line said, "United States Embassy." She could barely get the words out fast enough. "We need your help. I'm an American citizen, and my friend has just died. She is a mother of three small children, and she needs to get home. Please, please, we need to know how to get out of here and get back home."

"Please take a deep breath, ma'am. Slow down," said the reassuring voice.

"We need your help. Can you help us?"

"Yes ma'am. I'm a United States Marine officer. I can help you. I'm sorry to hear of the loss of your friend. Please tell me what happened."

"My nephew is a Marine." Her shaking subsided as she summarized all that had happened. He listened, and she gave him Edmundo's phone number so he could call back. Jenn was glad she had made the call and relieved to speak with someone who spoke English. He hadn't promised anything but said that he would have someone call her. She still didn't know what he could do to support the situation, but was grateful that someone else knew about the incident and might be able to help.

The next call was on the two-way radio from the Santa Elena Jaguar Inn to its Tikal counterpart. Jeff hadn't heard any specific news yet. Though looking at Val on the floor of the bungalow, Jeff suspected the outcome might not be good.

As they began to contact Jeff on the two-way, Jenn suddenly felt light-headed and nauseated. "Where's your restroom?" she asked, suddenly feeling the physical effects of the mental sickness she'd felt most of the morning.

After Jenn's calls, and despite hearing it would be of no assistance, Jenn and Edmundo decided to go to the other hospital in town and take a chance on obtaining a doctor's signature needed to move Valerie.

~~~

Jeff was sitting, standing, walking but mostly thinking as he tried to occupy both his body and mind in Tikal. The early-morning chaos of multiple voices in different languages, the blaring ambulance siren, and crackling of two-way radios were gone, and the jungle, though certainly not quiet, was once again void of manmade sounds. Jeff hadn't slept. There was no additional word on what had happened and little way of finding out. Each time he thought of Val on the floor, he felt sick to his stomach. There was still hope, and without word to the contrary, it kept him going.

The electricity had come back on at 4:30 a.m., which allowed Jeff to turn off his headlamp and made the process of gathering, stuffing, and closing our travel packs much easier. As he packed Valerie's and my bags, he kept watch for snakes or anything else that might have caused Valerie's condition. He didn't see anything.

Every vehicle entering the parking area brought the possibility of news, but few vehicles entered, and none had information regarding Valerie.

Jeff replayed details of the morning's incident. He wanted to think this was only a dream and recorded his thoughts in his journal: "It cannot be happening. I was hoping it was a dream, but deep down I knew it wasn't." With CPR started quickly, doctors nearby, and an ambulance taking Val to a hospital, Jeff tried to convince himself that all would be okay.

The early morning had a crispness to it, and the sun's first rays brought the jungle back to life. Jeff could hear two groups of howler monkeys in the nearby trees. Several exotic birds perched themselves above his head. A vulture chased an agouti in the parking lot, two brilliant redheaded parrots swooped down over his head, and a large multicolored toucan fluttered around the trees next to him. On any other day, it would have been a beautiful morning.

The ambulance returned with only two people, not the seven it had carried when it had left Tikal. As the two men exited the vehicle, their expressions said everything. Though they told

Jeff they didn't know the outcome, the solemn appearance on their faces didn't foster encouragement. They also told Jeff his wife would try contacting him over the two-way radio located in the restaurant. Jeff entered the restaurant at seven, when it opened, and waited about twenty minutes, when one of the workers told him there was a call for him.

"Hello, this is Jeff," he said into the two-way radio. "Hello, hello." There was no one on the other end of the line. A number of long minutes passed before he heard a voice on the other end.

"Pack everything and get here as soon as possible" were the first words from Jenn.

"What's the word, Jenn?" Jeff replied.

"She's gone," Jenn said in a softer tone.

"Oh, God." Jeff's heart sank into his soul.

Observing the expression on Jeff's face, the curious hotel workers did not need to hear the words themselves to understand that the news wasn't good.

"A van is on its way to get you," Jenn continued.

"I'll have everything ready." Jeff set the microphone down and walked out of the building. He gathered the bags he'd already packed and sat on the grass and cried. The sickness that had simmered in his stomach all morning had now moved to the rest of his body.

The group of French travelers who'd helped the night before came over to him, inquiring if he'd heard anything. The news of Valerie's death was a crushing disappointment to them, and they stayed, providing what comfort they could. While they were sitting outside, a small white van arrived in the parking area. To everyone's surprise, Julie was inside the vehicle. She looked withdrawn and saddened, and showed an unmistakable strain from the early morning's events.

"There was nothing more we could do," she said, shaking Jeff's hand and shrugging her shoulders.

For Jeff, the news was no better to hear the second time, shocking and even more difficult to understand. He hoped there'd be answers at the place where the white van would drop him off, but he wasn't completely sure.

As much as Jeff had looked forward to Tikal, he wanted to leave as quickly as possible. He wanted to see firsthand what was going on at the hospital, see Jenn and be at her side. At the same time, he didn't want to arrive. He wondered what it would be like to face me and what he should say. He'd thought about this on and off ever since his discussion with Jenn and he was no further along in coming up with some appropriate words of comfort than when he'd started thinking about it.

With a quick good-bye to the group gathered around him, Jeff threw the travel packs in the van and climbed inside.

The van, having just made the trip from Santa Elena, refused to start. Jeff experienced what we were dealing with at the hospital—encouragement, then disappointment. The consensus among the group was that a bad battery was likely the problem. The group began to push the vehicle, and, to Jeff's relief, the van's engine started.

Jeff settled into the van once again and looked out the window at the people who had just helped. Powerful emotions overcame him, feelings he would never forget. Here in this remote part of the world, he felt a sudden and unmistakable connection to the people who were now waving good-bye.

# Chapter 16

## Weathered Faces and Perplexing Voices

---

I stood up from the metal chair to use the bathroom and freshen up a bit. There had to be a restroom somewhere, and with no one to ask, I started walking toward the end of the room. The short journey served to answer several puzzling aspects of the night's activities. Two other similar three-sided low-profile cinder block rooms were adjacent to Valerie's room. They each contained a single lightbulb on the end of a flexible stand, and each had a metal table with a light-colored cloth draped lengthwise over it. Each of the cinder block rooms had a metal rod at the end, with a lightweight, yellowed curtain hanging from it. Above each room was an unsealed opening that struck a dramatic contrast between the bright-blue sky and the gray wall. Neither room was occupied.

At the end of the three rooms along the far wall was an elevated door. I turned to my right and pushed the door open. The substantial difference in height between the two floors would have never been allowed in most occupational settings. The door was heavily cracked, and peeling paint flakes covered its surface. The wood was warped, making it hang awkwardly on its hinges and unable to be fully closed. Any locking mechanisms had long since disappeared.

Looking inside the small rectangular room, I realized that the difference in floor elevation would have been the least of an inspector's concerns. On the far wall was another unsealed opening in the blocks, similar to the openings above the rooms I'd just walked past. Directly below was a toilet.

This was not a room in which to freshen up and think about the day's activities. Various bottles, cans, equipment, and paper products were crammed into every possible location. Cabinets were overflowing, and boxes and packages surrounded the toilet on three sides. Stacks of containers occupied both sides of the floor, forming a narrow path in the middle. Closest to the door were cartons of small medicine bottles containing varying amounts of liquid, and boxes of syringes, both with and without needles. Among those with needles, a few contained a protective sheath; most did not. It didn't appear the area was used as a disposal site for unwanted materials; it seemed to me the location was simply a convenient and frequently accessed spot for their medical supplies.

Pulling the door toward me, I stepped down from the elevated floor and looked back into the room. I couldn't help thinking the needles used on Valerie just hours before likely had come from this room. I wondered if one of these boxes once again contained the same needle.

The scene in front of me answered a few more of my questions and certainly reinforced that we were indeed in a remote part of the world. I should have realized the ambulance would be nothing more than a ride with fancy lights and a siren and that the hospital would not be a comprehensive facility with medicine and equipment, real doctors, and medical staff who would move into action to save Valerie's life. I should have known that hoping for an emergency medical helicopter or airplane was a hopeless fantasy.

I felt no anger toward the people or the facility. The environment in which we'd worked to save Valerie's life was far less than ideal, and I felt foolish I hadn't realized sooner how inadequate the conditions were or recognized that we wouldn't find a facility capable of handling the situation. As I was shaking my head about my lack of perspective of what might be available in the jungle, I realized I'd had to think that way. I'd needed optimism, to believe in a positive ending and that things would be all right. There'd been no alternative.

I returned from the restroom much more somber than when I'd left, and I wondered what would enter my mind next. I knew by now Jenn and Edmundo were likely finished with their calls and on their way back to the hospital. Jeff was probably on the road from Tikal. After speaking with Ludovic, I moved into position next to Val's side.

Not long thereafter, the female hospital attendant peeked her head around the curtain and motioned her arm toward two individuals standing just outside the room. One was an older man with an aged, slender body. His deeply wrinkled and darkened weathered skin showed the seasons of time. He did not smile, nor did he frown, and his mature and friendly look conveyed a sense of trust. He had the look of not wanting to interrupt my visitation with my wife and politely waited for my invitation to enter the room. He stood straight, but at maximum stretch, he was a full head shorter than I was. His clothes were dark and worn, he had an extended graying beard, and his thin, matted hair was pulled behind his ears. Behind him was a much younger man with a rounded face and plump figure. As I looked at him, he simply nodded and gave me a small smile.

Initially startled at their appearance, I motioned to them to enter the room, wondering why anyone would be here to see Val—or me, for that matter. As we stood facing one another, they exuded a calming presence, particularly the older man, and any wariness or apprehension I had quickly vanished. The older man opened his arms, and I instinctively accepted his hug, though I had no idea who these people were or what they were doing here.

I noticed the older person held a black bound book with no visible markings. The book, and the small cross on a thin chain around his neck, now visible next to an inside layer of clothing, suggested—or at least I assumed—that he was a man of God. Our communication consisted primarily of nonverbal hand gestures, somber smiles and nodding. It seemed they were not here to see me but to bestow a blessing on Valerie, and I did not question it further.

Valerie grew up in the Catholic Church and was proud of her Catholic roots even after she left Catholicism toward general Christianity. She had been active in our home church of St. Paul Lutheran and received frequent teasing—good-naturedly, of course—about switching religions.

"How does a confirmed Catholic become the director of youth ministry at a Lutheran church?" members would ask.

Val had taken it in stride, laughing with them and thinking nothing about it. Though they would tease, many told me the church was fortunate she'd accepted the unpaid time-consuming position.

Growing up in Central Minnesota meant there was a better than fifty percent chance you were Lutheran, as was the case for me. I was accustomed to feeling a closeness with fellow members, and the two people in front of me now, though unlike any church members I'd ever seen, somehow fit the mold. I had not yet wondered why God had allowed this tragedy to happen; these thoughts would set in later.

Given our Central American location, I assumed my new guests were likely Catholic, but I wasn't sure. At that moment, their religion was immaterial to me. They could have been most any faith, and I would have embraced them as distant brothers helping Valerie to another place beyond this world.

The older man opened that black book and quickly found the page he was looking for. He then started reading a passage aloud. Listening to him read in a language not my own was strangely comforting. As I focused my eyes on the words on the page, which were both upside down and written in Spanish, I tried to follow along. If the location of the man's hand was any indication of where we were on the page, we had reached a part that was in quotation marks and enclosed in a square. The men bowed their heads in what I thought was a prayer, and I joined them. I did not know if they were reciting the Lord's Prayer or not, but it really didn't matter. As they spoke Spanish words, I recited the Lord's Prayer in English. It seemed to work, as two languages joined as one.

The older man made a motion to the younger one, who immediately removed a small metal case from inside his multilayered clothing and opened it. The elder man reached inside and removed a slender vial from its velvet-lined resting place, and unscrewed its top. Placing his thumb into the vial, he removed a small amount of what appeared to be a clouded oily substance. After a few words, he rubbed his thumb in the sign of the cross on Valerie's forehead and spoke a few additional words.

The ritual was complete. They reassembled the vial's protective case, and the book gently closed. The older man made a deep bow in my direction, and they each gave me another peaceful hug before departing the room. The event was surreal in many respects. I returned to the chair next to Val and closed my eyes. A slight peace filled my mind for the first time that day.

"*Hola,*" was the next word I heard from the female hospital attendant as she motioned to a coffeepot in her right hand. I'm not a coffee drinker, and if I do have the occasional cup, the more I can make it not taste like coffee, the better. I knew the coffee would not be the sugary, creamy concoction I would like. However, the gesture was kind, and I nodded. She handed me a white Styrofoam cup with a very black substance in it.

Before I took a drink, and then again immediately after my first sip, it crossed my mind that in almost any other situation, I would never have drunk lukewarm flavored tap water anywhere in the country. *I don't care if I get sick,* I thought. Maybe it would take my mind off the situation for a short time. Perhaps getting violently ill was just what I needed.

# Chapter 17

## *Friend or Foe*

---

J enn and Edmundo returned from making calls and stated they'd gone to the other hospital. Just hearing they'd been to another hospital brought with it sadness and disbelief. The slight peace I'd felt after the religious ritual was over.

"Rod, I'm so glad Val wasn't taken to that place," Jenn said. "You wouldn't believe what we experienced there. As soon as we walked into the building, the smell hit us. The odor of the place was terrible."

Within the first few minutes of trying to locate a doctor, they'd seen both blood and vomit on the floor, and there'd been flies everywhere. She described a place packed with people, both sitting and literally lying on the floor right in the middle of the hallways. Jenn and Edmundo had been forced to step around and over people as they'd walked through the hospital.

"It didn't surprise me that the people there were very sick. You wouldn't go there unless you really needed to," Jenn said.

My wish that we'd gone to the other hospital in town was starting to diminish.

Even with Edmundo as a guide and translator, getting anyone to speak with them was difficult. Getting someone to produce the paperwork we required, particularly for someone located at another hospital, seemed impossible. The people they'd spoken with had told them to wait in the lobby, but after waiting in the reception area for a while and seeing patient after patient come through the door, they'd realized the assistance they were seeking would not be forthcoming anytime soon. Jenn and Edmundo had decided, if need be, they could always go back to the hospital, but they'd had enough. They'd left without making any progress toward getting a doctor to complete Val's essential departure paperwork.

"Jenn, two guys were here to see Val. I think they were from a local church. They performed some sort of ritual on her," I said.

"Really? I missed it? I asked Edmundo to see if he could locate a priest, but he didn't say anything about finding one. I really wanted to be here for that," Jenn said with genuine heartfelt disappointment.

"I'm not sure who they were," I said. "They may have heard it from someone else. There are a lot of people around here now."

We continued to talk and put the pieces of another broken plan back together. Our understanding was the ambulance drivers had brought us to a private hospital that specifically catered to people who could pay to see a doctor or have a particular procedure completed. The other hospital was open to anyone, regardless of one's ability to pay. That explained Jenn's description of a larger and more crowded facility in much worse shape than this one. I wondered, though, if the larger hospital, even with its odors and chaos, would have offered additional resources or would have made a difference.

Thinking about even the slightest chance for Val's survival at the other hospital made me shake my head and sigh. The devastation of having made a potentially fatal mistake was difficult to comprehend, and it weighed on my body.

~~~

Jeff arrived at the hospital sometime after nine in the white Jaguar Inn minivan. Though he knew Valerie hadn't made it, when we saw each other, our emotions let loose. We hugged, cried, and tried to comfort one another as best we could.

Companionship and strength in numbers were a benefit, and I was so very glad to have Jeff and Jenn at my side. We also hoped that Jeff's Spanish skills would increase our communication abilities.

When I was in the room alone with Val's body, I did not ask many questions. My mind became numb at the startling reality that I'd been unable to save her life. Together with Jeff and Jenn, the questions poured out. "Why did this happen? How could this have happened?" As we searched for answers, we knew, deep down, we wouldn't find any. Val's body still lay on the same table that we'd initially placed her upon. Little had changed as the day wore on, and the temperature and humidity rose. I felt a need to somehow rise above the numbness and once again think through the situation. The juxtaposition of vacation and Valerie's death was incomprehensible. Questions seemed to be abundant; answers were not.

We were hopeful the embassy and Edmundo's cell phone would help our cause, and later that morning, we spoke with a woman from the embassy named Ms. Clair. She seemed to understand our predicament and said what we needed to hear. However, Ms. Clair didn't know specifically what we needed to do nor what exact documents were necessary in order to leave the hospital. She did confirm there would be ample paperwork. She also made it clear we would not be leaving Guatemala anytime soon and going back through Belize wasn't an option, as all arrangements were required to take place in the country of death. She was unfamiliar with any funeral homes in Santa Elena, although she did know of some in Guatemala City. She reminded us it was Saturday, and answers to our many questions might not be easy to get. She would make some calls and get back to us.

"You may need an autopsy," Ms. Clair stated in a matter-of-fact tone just before she hung up the phone.

An autopsy? This was something I'd thought about previously, but with all the other things happening, conducting an autopsy here at the hospital hadn't crossed my mind. From the first sign that something was wrong with Val, I wondered what had caused her ailment. My initial thought was an animal bite. The jungle certainly had creatures capable of causing a severe reaction, but I had located no obvious signs of a puncture wound. An allergic reaction to food or some sort of respiratory contaminant seemed plausible, but I didn't know what those could be.

Over the course of the morning, both of these theories

seemed less and less likely. In discussions with Ludovic and Julie, nothing I described to them regarding Val and her medical history stuck out as a probable cause. Their best hypothesis was a brain aneurysm. I knew little about brain aneurysms, but with nothing else to go on, it seemed possible. I wanted to know specifically what caused Val's death, and to that end, an autopsy was necessary.

Less than three hours ago, I'd been thinking we had a good chance of making the morning flight out of Belize City. Those thoughts now were a distant memory. Valerie's body remained unmoved, and it probably wouldn't be moved from the hospital anytime soon. If Belize was no longer an option, I had no idea where we could, or should, take her.

"*Señor, señor. Teléfono,*" said the woman who'd previously showed me to the restroom and brought me warm coffee. I pointed to my chest, and the woman nodded. "*Sí.*" I had been on the phone several times already that morning, but no one had called for me. On the other end of the line was a man who was difficult to understand. The broken English and poor connection made it difficult for either of us to communicate. I could not hear his name and didn't want to ask him a third time, so I moved on. What I gathered during the conversation was he represented a funeral home and would be able to help us. I inquired if they could do an autopsy, and he stated they could most certainly perform the task. In fact, an autopsy would be required to get the final paperwork to depart the country. He told me they would start the arrangements and call us back shortly.

Just after hanging up the phone, several fundamental questions popped into my head. *Who was this guy? Where was he located? Was he representing a funeral home, or did he just know of a funeral home? What specifically was he arranging? How did he know about Val, our location, or me? Had the embassy called him?* I had no answers to these questions.

As one person presented possible solutions, another would summarily dismiss them. It seemed everyone was confused, and the situation would get even more complicated over the next few hours.

The portion of the hospital we were in had two outside doorways. One opened to the alleyway where we'd first entered. The other, across the hall from the cinder block rooms, opened into a small courtyard. Neither doorway contained an actual door. The courtyard was mostly unoccupied and was the place where Jeff, Jenn and I could find some quiet to gather our thoughts.

The recent telephone call from the man representing a funeral home was on my mind. We had tracked it down and now believed it came from someone named Fernando at a funeral home in Guatemala City. He'd stated that an autopsy would be necessary to leave the country. This was fine with me, as it would supply the answers to Valerie's sudden and unexpected death, and therefore the sooner the better.

After additional conversations with hospital staff, the three of us needed to talk things through, and we moved into the courtyard. This time, to our surprise, three men were standing there seemingly expecting us.

"We're from the funeral home," one of the men said in broken English.

"Did you call a while ago? Did someone contact you from another funeral home?" I asked. There was no outward reaction to my statements, and I turned to Jeff in a plea for translation. Jeff proceeded to select his words carefully and communicate the questions.

"No," was the eventual response from the man who had spoken previously.

"This isn't Fernando, is it?" I leaned over and asked Jenn.

"No, I'm quite sure of that, but I'm not sure who they are," Jenn said.

The next fifteen minutes were awkward at best. However, we eventually determined the three men were from a local funeral home. They would be glad to help us out, and they could provide everything we needed. We certainly needed assistance, that was true, but something didn't feel right.

"Do you know anything about an autopsy?" I asked, looking directly at the person who distinguished himself as the group's leader, knowing that Jeff would need to translate. Their confused looks did little to convey any confidence, and Jenn had had enough. She moved inside the hospital to speak with Edmundo, leaving Jeff and me to carry on the conversation.

"Sí," was the eventual reply from one of the men, with simultaneous nods from the two others.

"There's another call for you, Rod," Jenn said, sticking her head out the doorway.

"Great," I said, thinking at a minimum the phone call would provide a distraction from the confusing discussion with the men in the courtyard. Reentering the commons area, I noticed the number of hospital staff had again doubled in size; the news of a tall, blond, American woman's death had continued to spread.

I picked up the phone and prepared myself for the conversation.

"Hello, my name is Dr. Carlos from La Cumbre Funeral Home in Guatemala City," were the first words over the phone. *Yet another person from a funeral home—five within the last hour. What is going on here?*

"How did you hear about our situation? Did someone contact you?" I asked the person on the telephone.

"Yes sir. They did. Your embassy was in contact with us and spoke with one of my associates," said the man in English.

I wondered if Ms. Clair had contacted him.

Listening to the fundamentals of what he was proposing, I felt a need for someone else to hear what this man was saying. I handed the phone to Jenn.

"Jenn, there's a doctor from a funeral home in Guatemala City. Can you speak with him?" I asked.

"I've already spoken to La Cumbre—both Fernando and Dr. Carlos," Jenn said. "We just haven't had a chance to talk in detail, but I think these people know more about what to do than anyone else here."

Jenn took the phone, briefly spoke with Dr. Carlos, and then turned to me. "They need to make a few more calls and will call us back."

"What about the three guys out there?" I said, pointing in the direction of the courtyard. "Do they have anything to do with La Cumbre Funeral Home?"

"I don't think they do. They must have just heard of Val somehow."

"I agree," Jeff said. "I think they just heard stories and decided to come to the hospital. I can't really understand what they are saying we should do."

"It seems they nod in agreement to anything we ask. As far as what we should do, I'm not sure they really know," I said.

"What about an autopsy?" I asked Jenn. She only shook her head and shrugged her shoulders. Again, I had more questions to ask the man who was no longer on the phone.

Over the next few hours, more telephone calls and discussions made time move quickly, though one look into the room behind us clearly showed we'd made no practical or meaningful progress. The conversations moved in circles most of the time, and any advancements we thought we made provided only temporary satisfaction. Even answers to seemingly straightforward questions such as "What have you typically done in similar situations?" and "Is there a mortuary in this city?" provided no additional assistance.

A complex mixture of Spanish, French, and English filled the area, but by far the loudest conversations were between the Guatemalans as they appeared to be battling for some elevated position. In the midst of this mass of people—the ever-growing Santa Elena hospital staff; the mysterious official coroner who someone said was talking to the hospital staff again; the three local funeral home guys who'd appeared unsolicited, saying they would do anything we needed; Edmundo from the Jaguar Inn; the hotel manager from the Tikal Inn; Ms. Clair at the embassy; Fernando and Dr. Carlos at La Cumbre Funeral Home in Guatemala City; Ludovic, the French doctor; Jeff, Jenn and me—there had to be an answer to our problem.

Any particular person seemingly could provide a plan, but the issue as well as the number of people involved in each decision was growing exponentially. As divergent as this group was, we did have a uniform goal, a binding objective and a purpose to our gathering—Valerie.

We needed a doctor's sign-off on the death certificate, and if a doctor couldn't—or wouldn't—come to us, then we could take Val to him. In discussing this option with several hospital members, we learned this wasn't possible, and the hospital staff wouldn't allow it.

"There is another authorization we need," Ludovic said to Jeff, Jenn and me after talking with another group of hospital staff.

"Another release? Edmundo and I will try again at the other hospital to see if we can convince a doctor to sign the death certificate," Jenn said.

"No. This is a separate document. The attendant said there is another release necessary to allow the body to be moved," said Ludovic.

I shut my eyes, started shaking my head and sighed. I wished Ludovic was telling a bad joke, but his expression was anything but funny. We started yet another discussion and learned that we needed a high-ranking city official, someone equivalent to the mayor, to sign a transportation release prior to moving the body out of the city. Whether the transfer of Val's body was to another hospital or to a funeral home, presumably the one in Guatemala City, we needed the signed paperwork.

This was the first time we'd heard about the additional authorization. The response to our inquiry as to why we hadn't heard anything about this document before was dismissed outright and they hinted that we should've known about its necessity.

We heard a rumor that the person required to sign off on the transfer wasn't to be bothered today because he was attending a party. This was a setback and made us think about how many more signatures would be necessary and how long it would take to piecemeal the paperwork together.

Arguments between the hospital staff and others crowding the hospital corridors became commonplace. We could tell that many of the people we'd dealt with over the past six hours were hoping we could just leave and take all the others with us.

After another drawn-out discussion, Jeff turned to me. "Rod, they're saying they need your passports."

"They? Who are they?" I said.

"The guys we've been talking to in the hallway. One of them is from the local funeral home."

"Why do they need to see Val's passport?"

"Not just Valerie's passport—yours as well. They seem to think it will help with the paperwork." His voice was less than convincing, wondering how I would react. "I'm not sure we have many options left," he continued.

In our previous travels, Val and I had lost money and other personal belongings but had never lost our passports. We considered them our lifeline, and so I didn't take this request lightly. Listening to contradictory statements over the past number of hours also added to my reluctance. I didn't know if this effort regarding paperwork was any more or less credible than the other dozen or so attempts that we'd tossed about throughout the morning.

The people from the local funeral home were convinced our passports were integral to getting what we needed, but I didn't feel comfortable handing over our passports to the men who'd suddenly appeared in the courtyard. These men had managed to gain access to the hospital, inserted themselves into the situation, and now were apparently integral in getting Valerie home. I wasn't so much worried about fraud, document counterfeiting or identify theft, but the consequences of losing our passports would mean additional paperwork and, ultimately, more delay in leaving the country.

"Edmundo," I said, pulling him to the side with Jenn. "I'm entrusting you with these. Please use them as you need, but bring them back." Edmundo nodded in understanding. Looking him straight in the eye, I handed him the two passports with my left hand and simultaneously reached out with my right to seal the deal.

A number of men broke off from the larger group gathered in the common area, turned and walked out of sight.

# Chapter 18

## *The First Box*

---

The night's coolness had passed, and the steady advancement of the sun's warmth entered the hospital. The option of a local autopsy had also shifted, and Dr. Carlos's less-than-delicate comments reverberated in my head.

"Do not let them touch her. It would not be good if they did," Dr. Carlos said in a forceful and authoritative voice.

I wasn't sure what to say in response, and perhaps Dr. Carlos sensed my reaction and rethought his brash statement.

"The locals don't know what they are doing. Do not let them do the autopsy," he said in a conciliatory tone.

Though his voice became more pleasant, the words he used were not. My mind drifted to what might happen with heat and a dead body. *How long would it take to get to the funeral home in Guatemala City? What would happen to Val's body in the meantime?*

Ludovic, also cognizant of the situation, had already discussed the matter with several hospital attendants. It took more than a little encouragement for Ludovic to prevail in finding a temporary solution.

"I have arranged to move your wife to another section of the hospital," Ludovic told me. "There is air-conditioning there. It will be helpful if we move her soon," he said.

*There's another part to this hospital? With air-conditioning? Why didn't we know about this? What else does this secret part of the hospital have?* I thought as Ludovic explained the location of the room.

Shortly after 11:00 a.m., already eight hours after Valerie's episode began in Tikal, we had a plan to move her body to another room in the same hospital. We positioned a stretcher next to the metal table and moved her onto the rolling cart. Her body looked the same to me, but the thought of what warm weather would do to a dead body made me uncomfortable. Her skin was neither hot nor cool, and its color seemed grayer, but I did not stare.

I tried to stay focused on the conversation regarding what we needed to get Val's body to the next location, but my mind was wandering. As we were moving her body, a sense of foreboding came over me—one of absolute loss and emptiness. Even as people surrounded me, an incredible pain of loneliness enveloped me. Just as quickly, my mind turned to all the people in Valerie's past. I wondered what the loss would mean to our children and how they would get by in the future. What about Val's mother, my parents, her siblings . . .? The list seemed endless.

We went left out of the common area, down a short hallway, then right, up a slightly longer hallway, and then left again into the room. This room, and what appeared to be two similar rooms along the hallway, stood in stark contrast to the one we'd just come from. This room actually resembled a hospital room. The entrance contained a door that opened and closed, and the interior walls were finished, not simply painted exterior cinder-block walls. Valerie's new room had a large window on one side that contained glass. Cabinets and drawers lined the other two walls of the room. Nothing fancy, but compared to where we'd been, it was very upscale.

I couldn't believe we hadn't been taken to this area from the very beginning. Did the cabinets and drawers contain medicine, medical supplies, or life-saving equipment? If this room contained critical devices that could have helped, it no longer mattered. I no longer cared about anything that didn't help us with Val's current status. *Could have helped* was irrelevant. I was beginning not to care about many things.

"Rod, there's someone here to see you," Jenn said, reentering the slowly cooling room.

"Me? Who is it?" I asked.

"I'm not sure. Someone from the Guatemalan government, I think," Jenn said.

For the most part, I was thankful for all the assistance from people I'd never met before, but this seemed different. Maybe my mood had changed, or maybe it was the man's salesman-like look, but I saw no real purpose for him to be there, which made it difficult for me to listen to him.

He introduced himself as Cesar, and the card he handed me stated *Delegado Ofician de Información Turística, Aeropuerto*

*Internacional de Peten an Instituto Guatemalteco de Turismo.*
I didn't really know what the card meant but guessed from a
few words that seemed similar to English that he worked for
Guatemalan tourism somehow. As he spoke reasonably good
English, I wondered if his coming here was out of curiosity or
official business. The death of an American citizen under such
circumstances might not be good for tourism, and I wondered
if he was trying to assess repercussion from the incident.

After some discussion, my skepticism waned, as I decided
it really didn't matter why he wanted to speak with me. He
didn't ask questions, nor did he seem to be looking for answers.
Unfortunately, it didn't appear that he could help us either. I
thanked him for his time, but he persisted in asking to help.
I suggested he could help us find a place to stay, but I wasn't
sure where that would be. We shook hands, he departed, and
we never heard from him again.

～ⴰⴰⴰ～

"We have the paperwork," Jenn said, entering Val's new room
with as close to a smile as I'd seen all day.

"I thought someone needed to examine Val. Did the mayor
sign off? Which documents did we get?" I asked.

"The hospital staff stated they have everything they need,"
Jenn said.

"All of it? We can leave this place?" I asked in a cautious
but hopeful voice.

"I'm not completely sure what they have. All I know is they
just told me they have what they need to release Val."

"Maybe they just want us to leave," Jeff chimed in.

"I wouldn't doubt that." The day had been exhausting and

frustrating. With all the despair and grieving, even the smallest amount of good news provided relief.

A small group of people had gathered outside Valerie's room, and as I joined in the discussion, I could tell Ludovic was as relieved by the news as we were.

Edmundo was also near the group and gave me a broad smiled as I approached him.

"Here you are, Mr. Jasmer," Edmundo said as he handed me the two passports clenched in his right hand.

My trust in Edmundo was genuine, and his gesture completed the circle—my belief had not been misplaced. "Thank you, Edmundo," I said with an understanding nod as an even larger smile crossed his face.

We tried to connect the dots regarding the specific source of the documents, but there didn't seem to be one clear answer. We were more than ready to get moving and didn't want to ask additional questions of the hospital staff for fear they would change their minds or require additional documentation. We weren't going to wait around for that to happen. We had the papers that allowed Valerie's body out of the hospital, and out of the city, and did not spend additional energy determining exactly why.

The plan was to transport Val to La Cumbre Funeral Home in Guatemala City, and they could help us from there. Beyond this, we didn't know any details, but we viewed this as substantial progress.

The local funeral home trio was not happy that some big-shot city firm had closed in on their turf and taken their customer. Their hostility did subside somewhat when La Cumbre Funeral Home hired them to drive us halfway to Guatemala City.

We were pleased to have a door on our room as we sat with Valerie's body, waiting for the hearse to arrive. Just down the hall was the main entrance to the hospital, where Jenn had tried to get in. The area looked so very different now. The public freely entered and exited at will, and the dramatic increase of hospital staff provided an appearance of a proficient facility.

"Rod, we should put some different clothes on Val before we place her in the casket," Jenn suggested.

I hadn't thought about changing the clothes on Valerie's body and was grateful Jenn was thinking about such things. Though the details of what clothes Val wore seemed irrelevant, as opposed to comprehending the loss of her life, I understood Jenn's point.

"Sure, we can do that," I said.

We made our way past the people gathered in the lobby and then out the front doors to the graveled parking area. Our packs were in the white minivan Jeff had arrived in a few hours ago just outside the hospital's main entrance.

I hadn't spent much time outside the hospital, other than in the small courtyard, since I'd arrived. The day seemed particularly bright and hot. I spotted Val's pack in the van and started to open the zipper, then stopped. I held a zipper tab between my thumb and index finger, but my hand would move no farther. This was Valerie's pack, and it contained her belongings. She should be opening this up; I could not do it.

I turned around and looked at Jenn. "Can you pick something out? Whatever you think is appropriate will be fine. I can't do it." I walked to the other end of the van and looked at the now-open gates. They were the same wrought-iron gates Jenn had climbed over earlier that day. The area was all so different now.

Jenn turned to Jeff. "Did you pack everything? I can't find any of Val's underwear. I can't find much of anything with all their snorkel gear."

"I got what I could find. Maybe with all the commotion and overturned beds, I missed something, but I thought I got everything," Jeff responded.

"Well, I can't find any. I found a bra, but no panties. I'll just get one of mine," Jenn said mostly to herself. She decided it would be a good time to change her own clothes as well.

Back inside the lightly air-conditioned room, I noticed Jeff and Jenn looking at each other and making a few subtle gestures. As I started to remove Val's nightshirt, Jenn touched Valerie's shirt as well and held it down.

"Rod, we can do this," Jenn said, hesitantly looking into my eyes.

"I know you can. Thanks. I can do it and want to," I said. Though I had clearly struggled even selecting Val's clothes, this was something I needed to do. Val had a journey ahead of her, and I needed to get her ready for it.

"Are you sure? It may not look pretty, Rod. You were doing CPR for a long time," Jeff said.

I remembered several of my CPR instructors stating that significant damage to the skin and even broken ribs were possible. I prepared myself.

There was a large bruise and some blistered skin in the middle of her chest where the hours of CPR had taken their toll, but if any broken ribs existed, they were not noticeable. As we removed her remaining clothes, I noticed some fluid leaking from her, and her stomach was somewhat inflated. The sight did not bother me; she was as beautiful as ever.

None of us had ever handled a dead body. The situation itself was incredibly strange—not to mention the body was their good friend and my wife. There were no doctors explaining what we might experience, no nurses telling us what we should or should not do, no hospital orderlies to help. We just did what we thought was right. Val's body had cooled somewhat, but her skin was not cold. As I had experienced in the room in Tikal, gravity was the only force, other than our pushing and pulling, governing Valerie's body. Even for three of us, changing her clothes was not easy and took longer than expected.

Contrary to what one might reasonably expect of this task, there was something special about the moment. Jeff would later recall the occasion in his journal, stating, "I felt privileged to be there helping." I understand his reasoning and can appreciate why some cultures and customs bring the deceased and their loved ones together on a physical and personal level prior to burial.

Within twenty minutes, we heard an unusual amount of activity coming from the hospital's entrance and opened the door to see if the noise had anything to do with us, and of course it did. Down the hallway, through a set of glass doors, we could see several men removing what looked like a brown casket from an older hearse.

"I think our ride is here," Jeff said.

*Finally, things are coming together.*

None of us had paid much attention to the casket as a group of middle-aged men in tattered street clothes moved it from the vehicle to the waiting room. As the casket made its way into the room alongside Val, however, we noticed many things about it. For starters, it wasn't much of anything other than an old wooden box. The half-inch plywood container was widest at the shoulders with an elongated taper toward the feet and a shorter taper toward the head. At each end, the box was squared off, as if it hailed from an old Western movie. The reddish-brown-stained boards were heavily worn at their edges, and previous usage had scuffed and scraped its surfaces. We looked at each other and wondered if Valerie would even fit inside.

As one of the men we'd never seen before motioned to the wooden box and then to Val's body, we understood this wasn't some cruel joke. The container was indeed her next destination. Jenn, Jeff and I, along with two other men, lifted Val over the side and into the unlined, unpadded wood box with little room to spare. I hadn't noticed the cover until the men placed another separate piece of wood, cut into the same Western coffin shape, on top of the now-filled box. Without hesitation, question, or thought, the workers were handed—by a previously unseen person now in the room—a hammer and nails. What could we do but watch as the group of men secured the top of the box by placing used and bent nails into existing holes and pounding them down with a rusted hammer?

I tried to speak to Jeff and Jenn, but no sound exited my mouth. My mind whirled with uncertainties but did nothing other than fixate on the bewildering process taking place in front of us. I knew placing Valerie's body into a coffin would be required, and though I'd never really thought of what the casket would look like, I certainly had not been expecting anything close to this. As I stared at the coffin, astonishment battled with my unending sorrow.

# PART IV

*A Long Way to the Unknown*

# Chapter 19

## Misery Road

Val was still in the room but now inside a small plywood box. We were anxious to get on with what we were told would be at least an eight-hour drive to Guatemala City. Outside the hospital, the temperature was heating up rapidly, and it would hit the mid-nineties by midday.

Just after noon, a late-model Toyota pickup pulled into the hospital driveway and backed toward the entry. Jeff and I exchanged a glance as we noticed a blue tarp in the back of the small truck. I wasn't expecting a brand-new shiny black hearse, but I also wasn't expecting an open-ended pickup truck to back up as if they were loading supplies from a hardware store. The situation was hard to believe.

"What's this?" I asked as we moved to the warmer outside air.

"This will not work," Jenn said.

The general audience gathered near the hospital's entrance and the funeral home workers were oblivious to our reactions. Looking back toward the hospital, I watched a procession move through the crowd like a parade, with Val's coffin as the centerpiece in triumphant fashion. It appeared they'd conducted this exercise many times before.

The tailgate was lowered, the casket pushed in and the plastic tarp unfolded. The people in white hospital outfits were nowhere in sight, and there was no one to ask for assistance. Those individuals gathered outside were in street clothes and none were familiar, including the pickup's driver. We learned he just happened to have a slightly newer vehicle and was capable and willing to make the trip halfway to Guatemala City.

"This is good," said one of the men who'd just placed Val's coffin in the bed of the truck.

"No," Jenn and I said in unison.

"You can't even get the tailgate up," I said, lifting it slightly.

"Sí," he said with a nod, then moved to the other side of the vehicle and picked up a coiled rope.

I just couldn't have Valerie transported in the back of an open pickup with the tailgate down for the next eight-plus hours. We had many concerns, and the heat of the midday sun beating on a plastic tarp was one of them. They explained that the tarp would insulate the coffin from the elements. To my mind, it would work just the opposite way.

We tried to convey that we weren't looking for anything fancy nor were we seeking a more comfortable ride for us. Not having Valerie's casket hanging over the end of a pickup bed seemed like a reasonable requirement. They proudly showed us the inside of the cab, pointing out that the two small jump seats in the back would accommodate all of us, and that the truck was equipped with air-conditioning. We repeated our concerns about keeping Val's body as cool as possible, though our logic was neither understood nor well-received. The other people gathered outside were convinced this pickup was the best solution to our transportation needs and couldn't believe we were rejecting this fortunate option.

Though I don't believe they understood our reasoning, they agreed to arrange for another vehicle.

As the young driver with an empty payload and an unhappy face drove away from the entrance, all but three people understood the very best option for getting to Guatemala City was driving away as well.

Time passed slowly until the next vehicle arrived, and though it was indeed black, it also was not what we were hoping for. An old Chevy Suburban with numerous scrapes and dents began backing toward the hospital door. The front doors had the word *Funeraria* (Funeral Home) painted on them. The red-lettered words had likely been a proud and bold symbol at one time; now they were badly sun-faded and cracked. The Suburban had seen its share of years and miles, and I wondered if it would even make the trip.

With the day slipping away and no other reasonable options, this would have to do. Looking in the back of the Suburban, we knew it would not be easy to fit us and the coffin, and adjustments would be required. We first removed several old boxes containing miscellaneous parts, tools and equipment from the back of the vehicle. Next, we took out the backseat. The middle row of seats operated independently, so we folded the left side down as far as it would go and then wedged the coffin into the back of the Suburban diagonally. We gathered our travel packs from the van and placed them around the casket. The loose spare tire we repositioned against the coffin, and after some additional rearranging, we managed to close the door.

Time to leave a place that we'd never expected to be. Edmundo had paid the hospital bill before I even inquired about it. I was grateful for this, as I wasn't sure what form of payment they would take and not even sure if the Guatemalan quetzals were in our travel packs or still in the room at Tikal. Jenn already had Edmundo's e-mail address, and I told him I would repay him when I got home.

Ludovic had courteously stayed by our side, and it was now time to say good-bye to him as well. I could sense he was more than ready to leave the hospital. We were all ready to move on, wherever that might be. I was incredibly thankful for his help, but his service and my gratitude went well beyond that. He had made a choice to be there; his unquestioning commitment and his individual empathy had brought us to this point. I assumed Ludovic would return to Tikal via Edmundo's small white van. I wondered if it would require another push to start.

The Suburban's engine started, and Jeff, Jenn and I climbed into the vehicle. Jeff and Jenn sat together on the unfolded portion of the middle seat alongside the foot end of the coffin. The driver's assistant sat in the far back by the coffin without a seat, with the driver and me in the front.

As we drove out of the hospital gates, I turned and nodded at Jenn and Jeff and gave them a small smile. The situation was far from ideal, but we had moved beyond any best-case scenario long ago. I was glad Val's body was inside the same enclosure we were in.

We soon realized the air-conditioning was not working, which was disappointing though not surprising. We resigned ourselves to just rolling windows down and letting the hot air move in and out.

We had gone only a few slow miles through town when we stopped for gas, a restroom break and an opportunity for our two-person crew to purchase a number of small supplies. Beyond their hearing distance, I turned to Jeff.

"They couldn't have filled up the gas and bought snacks beforehand?" I wondered if this break was part of the "estimated" eight-hour trip.

The men returned, and we were on the move again. We were not racing in any sense of the word but traveling a consistent speed along narrow and curvy but reasonably maintained paved roads. Within an hour into the drive, the inevitable consequence of driving an older vehicle in the Central American rural countryside showed itself when a loud pop broke the silence followed by the unmistakable sound of loose rubber flapping against the pavement.

The driver pulled onto the narrow shoulder of the road, allowing just enough room for other vehicles to pass. The spare tire Jeff and I had moved several times to position the casket in the back of the vehicle now came in handy, though we wondered if it had sufficient air pressure to hold the heavy vehicle.

During our travels toward the city, we had noticed scattered tree branches alongside the road, and we now understood their use. While our driver looked for the jack around Val's coffin, his assistant cut branches from nearby trees and placed them in bundles about twenty-five yards in front of and behind our disabled vehicle as a sign to others of our misfortune.

Our transportation plan called for the local funeral home workers to drive us approximately halfway to Guatemala City to meet representatives from La Cumbre Funeral Home at approximately three thirty in the afternoon. Here we were sitting on the side of a remote Guatemalan road in the heat, only an hour from our starting point. At this moment, no one was thinking we would be early.

After a twenty-five-minute delay, we found ourselves traveling along an even narrower road. There was no dashed yellow center line or white lines identifying the road's edge. When encountering another vehicle, both drivers had to slow down and maneuver past each other with caution. Fortunately, we saw few other vehicles.

On this stretch of road, the landscape consisted of lush green vegetation and several round-top mountains covered in thick layers of vegetation that rose distinctively from the otherwise flat ground. We passed only a few structures, most all of them oddly shaped and built of dissimilar materials.

We rounded yet another curve in the road, and as we approached a group of small dwellings, the driver suddenly turned off into a dirt driveway and stopped next to one of the structures.

"Why have we stopped?" Jeff asked in his best Spanish.

I was agitated. Why would we stop in the middle of nowhere when we needed to meet the other group?

"To service the tire," said the driver as he exited the vehicle.

A middle-aged man and his young son, who looked to be about eight, greeted the two men from the Santa Elena funeral home. The conversation started swiftly and included mostly nods of acknowledgment from the skinny, grease-covered but bright-eyed man. As the discussion continued, it seemed to be about more than fixing a flat tire. The three of us decided to get out, stretch our legs and maybe see if we could find out what was going on.

"I think they're negotiating a price," Jeff said, trying to hear the discussion.

"Tell him I'll pay for the tire. That isn't our biggest concern right now," I said, frustrated. Before we could intervene, the conversation ended. The man and his son immediately moved into action.

The tire shop was a small three-sided building behind some shrubs just feet from what appeared to be their house and no more than thirty feet from the main road. A Goodyear service center it was not, but the heavily worn and dirty equipment did the job. The father and son worked as a team, as fast as anyone I have ever seen repair a tire.

I saw a stump a short distance away and sat down. Here I was off to the side of a narrow road in the middle of a never-ending sea of jungle vegetation. I looked at the aged Suburban and shook my head. Valerie's body was in that broken-down vehicle in a wooden box. Feelings of disbelief once again struck me. *It just can't be. How could any of this have happened?* I became dejected and closed my watering eyes.

Jeff and Jenn were on the other side of the vehicle, and from their vantage point, they could see a group of three women standing just behind and to the side of the house. The women were looking at Jeff and Jenn and giggling.

"I don't like this," Jenn said to Jeff. "They're laughing at us."

"How would they know our situation?" Jeff said.

"They do know what's going on," replied Jenn. "They think it's funny. We need to get back on the road."

Though I didn't see money change hands, our driver must have paid the man who'd fixed the tire. I looked in my wallet and noted I had a single one-hundred-dollar bill, a ten, and a few ones. I had no idea where my Guatemalan currency was. If this had been our final destination, or if I knew I wouldn't need money for some other unforeseen event, I would have gladly given the hundred dollars to the man and his son. I thought of the traveler's cheques that were hopefully still in my pack and of my credit card, but knew they were useless here.

I pulled out the ten-dollar bill and offered it to the man and his son. There was a slight hesitation in his gesture. He had fixed the tire for the negotiated price. I could see his pride, but he had a family, and in 2004, ten US dollars were equivalent to eighty Guatemalan quetzals. From what we'd heard from others, a typical individual in Guatemala earned an average of thirty-eight quetzals per day; indigenous people, like our tire-fixing friend, would make significantly less. Two to three days' wages was not something to pass up, and he took the money. As our driver and his companion made their way to the vehicle, we thanked the man and his son for their wonderful work—Jeff and Jenn in Spanish and I with a direct English "thank you."

I hadn't wanted to stop but was now grateful to be back on the road in less than a half hour with a usable spare tire.

The temperature continued to climb, and the wind coming through the windows did little to cool us off. Looking into the sky, I hoped the sun would lose some of its power soon.

We were on a slow but steady pace along some lonesome road in Guatemala when another bang hit our ears. The noise was much louder than the previous one, and the three of us let out a collective sigh of exhaustion. The driver again pulled to the side of the road, and we got out to survey the damage.

The rear passenger tire had blown out so badly that the cords were visible through the gaping hole. It appeared unfixable.

This time we'd stopped along a dangerous curve and, as before, cut and placed tree branches on the road. The replacement process was similar to the first, though removing the tire did not go as well. The jack wasn't working properly, and the vehicle's awkward position and the tight lug nuts all proved challenging.

Jeff and I assisted in trying to replace the tire, and after two other vehicles narrowly escaped hitting us, Jenn grabbed some tree branches and moved to the road to alert oncoming traffic of the peril just ahead of them. Beyond trying to change a tire and having Val's body in the heat, the sounds of hard-braking vehicles and their blaring horns added to our anxiety. Another thirty-five minutes or so later, for the fifth time since leaving the hospital, we were again on our way.

Our driver used his cell phone repeatedly during the trip. It seemed odd to be getting coverage in such an isolated part of the world. I had trouble with coverage at my house, but here, in remote north-central Guatemala, apparently coverage abounded. That is, until I suggested we call the people we were meeting from La Cumbre to tell them we were going to be late.

"No," the driver said as he pointed to his phone, showing me he no longer had service.

Time stood still during the remaining part of the trip. Our

sluggish travel was agonizing, driving slowly on the open road, presumably in an effort to not blow another tire, then even more slowly through small towns along our path. Each little village was full of people on this late Saturday afternoon. In several instances, pedestrians completely surrounded our vehicle as if a major sporting event had just concluded and we were located just outside the main gate. Without traffic lights or pedestrian walkways, we crept along as people moved past in every direction. I wondered what they thought about us—three fair-skinned, fatigued people in a large vehicle with *Funeral Home* written on both doors.

We no longer had a spare tire, and the heat was intense. We didn't know where we were, where we were specifically going, or what time we would arrive. I tried not to look at my watch (which I found in my travel pack Jeff brought to the hospital) because the past eight times I had, the time had barely changed. *I'm not going to look,* I would tell myself. Then holding out as long as I could without looking generally meant an eight-to ten-minute interval had passed.

*What if we get another flat tire? I guess we could remove the tire, hitch a ride.* I needed to occupy my mind, so I thought of such things. *It's really been a while now since I looked at my watch. Okay, good, that was another nine minutes.*

"How much longer?" This time actual words came out of my mouth.

"Thirty minutes," said the driver.

Jeff only shook his head. He had asked this question about forty-five minutes ago, and the driver had given the same answer.

"Another thirty minutes?" Jeff said.

We wondered if he had ever driven this road before, or if he even knew where he was going.

"Can we call them? We should call whomever we are meeting and tell them we are still on our way," Jenn said to the driver.

"No battery" was the response, but this time he didn't show us his phone.

We entered another village, and again our pace slowed considerably as we maneuvered through the congested streets. In what appeared to be the center of the town, we abruptly pulled off into a large gravel parking lot. Several one-story buildings surrounded the parking area, one of which appeared to be a restaurant.

"Is this the place?" Jenn asked no one in particular, and received no reply.

Though I'd looked at my watch a hundred times, I didn't recall the time we arrived. Jeff would later tell me it was after five.

On the far right side of the graveled area, we could see a standard dark-gray hearse. In stark contrast to our attire, two men in suits and ties leaned against its side panels, one with his arms crossed, the other with his hands pushed deeply into his pockets. Neither man was smiling.

It took little time for our drivers and the drivers from the other vehicle to engage in a thundering conversation. Having become accustomed to this form of banter, we tried to ignore the highly spirited discussion and only watched and listened from a distance. I was more interested in stretching my legs and getting away from the plagued Suburban.

Looking more closely at the shiny hearse from Guatemala City, I noticed a casket inside. We needed to transfer Valerie's body. The wooden box was only a temporary container that the men from the local funeral home would take back with them and use for their next job. I thought about what we needed to do and started pacing around the lot.

I could not recall a time in my life when I did not want to see Val—until now. I hoped they didn't need me to help move her; I wasn't sure I could do it. The sensation of not wanting to see Valerie was strange.

"Jeff," I said, trying to get his attention without completely interrupting his conversation with Jenn. As Jeff approached, I wondered if I could ask him to do this. "I can't do it, Jeff. I can't help transfer the body. I just can't," I said in a rush.

I didn't want to know what fourteen-plus hours of not breathing looked like, what bouncing around in an unprotected wood box would do to her, nor what high temperatures did to a lifeless body. I feared my efforts to preserve her body had been ineffective, and I did not want to see the results of my inadequacies. The sense of failure was real, and there was nothing I could do about it.

"Rod, it's done," Jeff yelled across the parking area where I'd been walking aimlessly in circles.

"That was fast," I said, though no one could likely hear me. With the transfer complete, I tried to put thoughts of the condition of Val's body out of my mind; however, suppressing them wasn't easy.

Our first drivers were paid, and they left. Once again, our fate was in the hands of complete strangers.

"We can only fit one person in the car," stated the taller of the suited men. "We did not know we were picking up three people, so we brought this smaller vehicle."

"We've been together the entire time," Jenn said.

"We all need to go together," I said, bewildered at his matter-of-factness.

As we discussed the situation, Jenn moved to the back of the hearse, looked in, and then began to crawl inside to see if she could fit. She barely fit, but if she wedged her body between the casket and the window, she thought it might work.

"No," said the other man standing in front of the vehicle after noticing Jenn maneuvering into the back. He motioned her to exit, grabbed her ankles, and began pulling her out.

We argued our case, and eventually one of the men got back into the car to make a phone call. At least ten minutes passed before he exited the hearse.

"You can go with us," he said, pointing to me. "You two can take the bus and meet us at the funeral home later."

We suspected we were approximately halfway to Guatemala City, but that was merely a guess. We knew we were likely somewhere mid-country, probably not close to the border and over a half-day's drive from Santa Elena. Typically, tourists would have a guidebook, a map of the area, and currency corresponding to the country. We had none of these. We asked about our location, but their response was indecipherable, and the conversation became confusing to all of us.

We didn't like the option they proposed, but the two people in suits and ties were steadfast. For a moment, we prepared to accept the possible outcome of splitting up. Maybe taking a bus wouldn't be that bad. Jenn and Jeff would need to find a bus station, locate the correct bus, ride four to six hours, likely stopping in every small town along the way, and then somehow meet up with me in the largest city in Central America late at night.

"Where could we catch the bus?" Jeff asked. The taller of the two men pointed and began giving complex directions. That was the tipping point. I thought about not having them by my side, and separating became absurd. I didn't want Jenn and Jeff to try to find a bus in a strange town and then try to locate me who knows where. We'd come into the country together, and we were staying together.

I didn't say anything as I grabbed a travel pack and shoved it on top of the casket.

"No," was the only word I could understand from them, but by this time I had the third bag in my hands and was cramming it into the hearse. They barely fit, and as the last pack pressed tightly against the window, I started to maneuver myself into the back.

"We're all going together," I said, squeezing my body alongside the casket. I wasn't coming out, and without any additional words, the drivers understood.

Jenn and Jeff did not hesitate and filled the two positions remaining along the front bench seat. That left the non-driver no choice but to crawl in the back opposite me on the other side of Val. With some jostling of position, we set off.

Even with my limited view, I sensed we were traveling quite quickly. The driver was not afraid to use the horn to honk at the people using the road as their personal walking path. As we moved south, the distance between villages lessened. During the unpopulated stretches, the driver would push the pedal down, and though I couldn't see the speedometer, unfortunately for Jenn and Jeff, they could. The gauge became a magnet for their eyes. On several occasions, the old overloaded hearse thundered along the narrow curvy road at over one hundred miles per hour.

We traveled miles without a sound. No radio, no discussions—just the engine and the occasional sound of tires screeching and gravel flying into the wheel well as the driver dozed off and the right front tire exited the pavement. Jeff and Jenn were concerned the first time this happened, and much more so when he nearly drove completely off the road a second time. My current position allowed for only limited movement, and my vision was restricted to a portion of the side window. I was content not knowing the details of something I could do nothing about.

We were near the equator, which meant the daylight hours were similar to that of the nighttime hours. In my native state of Minnesota, when the temperature was as warm as it was in Guatemala, it would mean that daylight would extend past ten at night. The fact that the sky was already getting dark and the temperature was still very warm added to my internal confusion.

The onset of dusk combined with a population increase did not make the situation any better. Our driver suddenly swerved to miss a man walking along the road, jarring loose one of the packs. The piece of luggage moved quickly along its path of least resistance and hit my fellow rearward-riding companion squarely on the side of the head. What might have been funny in another situation was not.

"Please, God, let us make it," Jenn said, turning to Jeff after our third near miss.

Jeff, too, was more than a little concerned about the ride and wondered how the newspapers would describe the cover story of four Americans and two Guatemalans found dead in a small overturned hearse alongside the road. Jeff couldn't come up with a good explanation, but it did occupy some of his time.

It had been over three hours since we'd seen the sun, and only now did it seem as if we'd reached the outskirts of a larger city. The remaining forty-five-minute drive seemed to take us deeper and deeper into the bowels of a never-ending metropolis. As the night darkened and the dirt and grime increased, the number of people on the streets significantly decreased.

*Where could we possibly be going? This is a better vehicle than the one we started out in, and the drivers have suits on, but what if the drive was all a show? Why are we heading into a run-down residential neighborhood? Where is everyone? What is this place?*

A day without food, little water, and a fatigued body has a way of making one's mind wander. At times, a crisis can refocus energy into other matters. On that particular day, my human needs had several other items competing for attention. The disparity between physical demands and mental perceptions can be great; in my mind, they now merged into a jumbled mess. I was in shock and grieving, but also hungry, thirsty, frustrated and confused.

Night and a strange city typically do not mix well. After hours of riding in a cramped space, only seeing glimpses of our surroundings, I began to think that maybe this was some sort of elaborate ruse or even imaginary. *Could the drivers be taking us to a location other than a funeral home? Are we in danger? Is any of this real?*

The day's brightness was gone, replaced by an indisputable darkness. I was jammed between a coffin containing my wife, travel packs and the side panel of a hearse. Many things seem more dramatic at night, and I was contemplating the worst of them.

# Chapter 20

## *Guatemala City*

---

We pulled into what appeared to be an underground parking garage, then traveled along its concrete maze before the ever-present sound of the engine ceased. We had arrived, but we didn't know where. It took some time to exit the hearse, and once I was out, it felt good to move unimpeded. As we regained full function of our bodies, we noticed a flurry of motion in this underground world. Numerous other hearses were scattered around the parking area, and people, all in the same dark-blue suits as our drivers, were everywhere. The activity level wasn't what we'd expected at a funeral home at ten fifteen on a Saturday night.

"Where are we?" Jenn asked a uniformed individual moving toward us from among several parked vehicles.

"This way," said the man, motioning us away from the congestion.

"Where's the car going?" I asked. "We have our packs inside."

"*Señor*, please, this way," he replied. "We will take good care of your belongings." Though his assurance seemed sincere, I questioned if we should leave our items and Valerie behind. We followed his instructions and moved up a flight of stairs.

He escorted us along a hallway and past a number of offices and eventually seated us at a desk, where another individual seemed to be expecting us. I thought this had to be Dr. Carlos, the funeral home's director.

"We are prepared to help you with anything," stated the person I believed we'd spoken with several times earlier in the day. "What are your needs? La Cumbre Funeral Home can help you."

His ability with the English language and personal skills were not as keen as I remembered them to be on the phone. The time was late, and maybe he was as tired as we were.

"What would you like from us?" he said.

The words were unexpected. I knew he would have questions for us, but not these. His words were neither helpful nor comforting, and the manner in which he engaged us seemed as if we'd just entered a timeshare negotiation.

*What do I need? I need not to be here. I need my wife not to be dead. I need to know when Valerie can leave this country. We all need sleep, food, and something to drink. We're not here causally shopping funeral homes. We were sent here, and I don't know really where the hell we are or why we are here.* These were my first thoughts. I suppressed them and tried to push them from my mind.

"I'm not sure what we need. I was hoping you had those answers. We've discussed our situation several times already today," I said.

"I don't think this is Dr. Carlos," Jenn said, leaning over to me. "This is someone who works here." She seemed as frustrated as I was.

"Is Dr. Carlos here?" Jenn asked the man across the desk.

"Dr. Carlos is not here tonight. He would like to speak with you on the phone," the man replied.

"Is Fernando here?" Jenn asked.

The man looked up from the papers in front of him; he had a puzzled expression.

"*Sí*. Fernando is here. You have already met him when you first arrived. He will be back shortly."

The three of us exchanged glances as none of us remembered meeting Fernando.

"If you would like, I can see if Dr. Carlos can speak with you now," he said as he picked up the telephone and started to dial.

The phone conversation with Dr. Carlos was much more calming. He assured us over the speakerphone that Valerie's body was in good hands, and his people knew what they were doing. He was clearly good at his profession, and he seemed, more than most, to understand our situation. He went on to explain that the embalming process would begin tonight or early tomorrow and that Valerie's body would be completely prepared for transport back to America.

That was good news, a small victory, but like many other small successes, they paled in comparison to the overall subject matter. We were talking about properly packaging and delivering my dead wife's body. As we discussed their process, my despair returned and I struggled to subdue it.

"When will the autopsy occur?" I inquired, hoping to find out the reason for Val's unexplained passing as soon as possible.

"No, no. You should have that done when you get home," was his immediate response.

"But I thought we needed one now," Jeff said.

"I remember you saying we didn't want the local funeral home in Santa Elena to conduct the autopsy, but Fernando said an autopsy was required," Jenn inquired.

"Won't the embalming process interfere with an autopsy?" was my next question, overlapping Jenn's.

"No. Believe me, you don't want that done here," was Dr. Carlos's response. "We will do a minimal embalming on her to allow for an autopsy in America."

None of us knew what "minimal embalming" meant, and on any other occasion, the phrase would require more explanation, but we did not request elaboration. Once again, we were conflicted, confused, exhausted and frustrated.

*Why had they told us on several occasions we would need an autopsy prior to leaving the country?* I wondered. What we thought was absolute fact was summarily dismissed with another absolute truth.

"So we really didn't need to come all the way to Guatemala City, find a larger funeral home, and have an autopsy completed in order to get Val home?" As I voiced the question, Dr. Carlos began talking.

"Sorry, I need to be on my way now. I will see you tomorrow. I assure you, my staff will take good care of you." As quickly as the conversation had started, the doctor ended the call.

The La Cumbre representative sitting behind the desk had no reaction to the conversation and continued typing on his computer. From time to time, he would stop and ask a question, then continue typing.

"Next you must select a casket," he said.

"Now?" Jeff asked. The most even-keeled person was starting to feel the effects of the day.

"Yes, yes, of course," was the reply, as if our reaction was absurd.

We exited the office and followed the man to make our casket selection. The funeral home was much larger than the hospital. We made our way down one hallway, up and down stairs, past several other hallways and meeting rooms. On this late Saturday evening, a number of visitations were taking place, and as we passed these proceedings, we noticed everyone was dressed in their finest clothes. A strong feeling of being out of place hit me. The sharply adorned room contained men in suits and ties and women in black dresses and veils. In contrast, we were unshowered, unshaven Americans in grimy T-shirts and stained shorts, looking beat and worn down. The irony of a complete cultural reversal resonated deeply.

They showed us many caskets, the differences of each explained in full by our businesslike tour guide. It appeared he'd given this speech more than once, and we were happy when his cell phone rang and he needed to excuse himself. Almost instantly, there was another person to fill his place.

"The light-gray casket here or the white casket around the corner are really the only caskets to meet your needs," said our newest assistant, "since you require a special sealing mechanism for air travel."

*Why didn't he just tell us that in the first place? Why did he show us all these other caskets if only two would work?* I thought, though I resisted the urge to say it aloud.

"Okay, I guess the white one," I said without much deliberation.

"Great choice. It's one of our most expensive models. I'm sure you will like it," he responded with a smile.

The setting was surreal, and I was only now beginning to absorb what had just transpired. We were in a large Guatemalan funeral home, and a man dressed in his Sunday best was telling us we had just selected a fine casket. Many times during the day, the entire episode had felt like a dream, but at this moment, any veil of delusion lifted. I suddenly missed Valerie like never before. Each decision and event leading up to her death played in my head. I thought about how I would tell others the news and the fear and sorrow it would surely invoke in them. Our current setting made it abundantly clear that I had been unable to save her life. Though impossible to imagine yesterday, this stark reality became concrete in the form of a white casket I'd just selected. Jeff and Jenn appeared to be having a similar emotional experience.

We started back to the same office, this time taking a more direct route, and found ourselves again with the man who had initially started our tab.

"How would you like to pay for this?" he asked.

"All I have is a credit card," I said, digging into my wallet. I pulled out the card, and he gladly accepted.

He left the room and returned shortly, handing me my card and a receipt. "Fernando would like to talk with you," he stated.

"Great, we have many questions for him as well," Jenn said.

Fernando entered the room and moved behind the desk that appeared to be his.

"I noticed you have turned down the autopsy," said Fernando after shaking our hands and looking at us somewhat suspiciously.

"We want one, but not here. We just got off the phone with Dr. Carlos, and he said an autopsy was not necessary for the transport back to America," I said.

"But why not? What is your reasoning? Do you not think we can perform such a service?" said Fernando in a voice that had become increasingly stern. "You do not believe my country is capable of such things? Is that correct?"

The meeting had turned sour. While we'd believed our conversation with Dr. Carlos just minutes ago had been good, the discussion with Fernando had taken an unexpected deviation and was going downhill quickly. He spoke with a heavy Spanish accent, though his questioning and intensity were unmistakable.

"Is there another reason for evading the autopsy perhaps? Maybe you are hiding something?" Fernando pressed on.

The three of us looked back and forth at each other, wondering what to say. In our current states, we probably looked like we were guilty of something.

Fernando did not wait for a response from us. "Perhaps the authorities can sort out your resistance to know the truth," he said sternly.

"We're going to jail," Jenn said under her breath.

It did feel as if we were in some serious trouble, and I wondered who would be able to help us out of this.

"One moment, please," Fernando said as someone entered the room and requested his attention. Fernando moved to the back of the room and started another conversation.

"What's he saying?" I asked in a quiet voice, turning to Jeff and Jenn.

"We may need to get in touch with the embassy again," Jenn said, struggling to think of ways out of our quickly eroding situation.

"Jeff, are we understanding him correctly? We need to tell him the official in Santa Elena already inspected the incident and cleared us—me—of any wrongdoing. Can you talk to him in Spanish to see if he can understand us better?

"We must have offended him for saying we didn't want an autopsy conducted here," Jeff said.

Maybe Fernando overheard our muted conversation, maybe he was just playing with us, or maybe he realized the lateness of the day and decided it was time to move on, but upon his return, and before we could answer his barrage of questions, Fernando changed to another topic.

"Where would you like the body shipped?" Fernando asked in a matter-of-fact tone.

I wasn't sure how to respond and looked at both Jeff and Jenn. With caution, we answered his last question without elaboration. Although he didn't use the accusatory tone from earlier, the accusations lingered unmistakably in the room.

After a few additional questions, Fernando stood. "That is all. Thank you for using La Cumbre Funeral Home."

He shook our hands and he was gone.

❧

I hadn't seen Val's body for a while, and after the casket selection trip and the intense questions from Fernando, I needed to see her. Conciliatory words from funeral home staff saying that everything was fine did little to satisfy me, and after some persuasion, they reluctantly agreed that we could see her but requested a little time to set up a room.

I remembered not wanting to help transfer Val's body between caskets several hours ago, but now I needed to see her, regardless of her condition. The viewing was relatively quick, and for the most part, I just needed to confirm she was indeed there and nothing else had happened to her. I said a short prayer and told her how much I loved her and that I missed her already.

We were glad to have contacted Ms. Clair from the embassy earlier and not relied on Mr. Cesar from the Guatemalan tourism bureau to get us a place to stay. La Cumbre arranged for one of their drivers to take us to a nearby hotel, and on the way he apologized that the hotel they'd planned to take us to was full. He assured us the alternative hotel was in a nice location, and he dropped us off at La Casa Grande Hotel. Neither the specific location nor the hotel itself made any difference to us. We were glad to have rooms.

After checking in, Jeff helped me carry Val's bags to room number twenty-six. Jeff had asked the hotel receptionist if they had any food available, and as expected, they did not. We settled into the rooms just before one o'clock on Sunday morning. Approximately twenty-two hours had passed since I'd been awakened in Tikal, though time's relevance in my head made it seem both twenty-two seconds and twenty-two lifetimes ago. After Jeff left the room, exhaustion invaded my body. We hadn't eaten a single thing the entire day, but I was no longer hungry.

As I lay in bed, I knew sleep would not come easily. My toe hurt, and I realized I'd struck it on something as we'd left the bungalow. By examining the injury under the bathroom light, I saw it was no small scrape. The skin was torn, and the toe was red and swollen. The toenail would eventually blacken and would become a daily reminder of the night's events. It would not be until October, six months later, that the blackened mark worked its way to the end of the toenail.

Except for business trips or the odd jaunt to visit a friend or family member, this was the first night in roughly seventeen years Val was not lying next to me in bed. The words "till death do us part" came to mind, although I very much considered myself still married to her. My gaze moved to Valerie's travel pack in the corner of the room. I felt compelled to touch Valerie's belongings she'd packed just days ago. I again got up from the bed, opened her pack, and looked at her stuff. They'd taken on new and more significant meaning than they otherwise would have. *I remember when we bought this. Didn't one of your sisters give you this?* The items brought with them a comforting closeness, but it didn't last long as soon the wonderment of holding her possessions turned.

*How could this happen? Why did it happen? Why aren't you here with me?* As I sat on the tiled bedroom floor, I began to cry as many of the ever-building emotions came out for the first time.

My thoughts returned to the first sound I'd heard from Val's mouth the night before. I had initially thought the sound was the start of a nightmare. The more I thought about this, however, it really wasn't the same sound at all. Any sound from Val at night and I immediately assumed the noise was the result of another nightmare. I made a mental note to ask our family doctor, as well as whoever would conduct the autopsy back home, about a possible connection between the nightmares and her death.

I cried, grieved and felt a deflating sorrow, and my mind whirled to many topics. I wondered what this all meant and what the possible repercussions of Valerie's passing would be. Though I tried, I could not focus on any subject very long. It felt as if my life would never be the same again, and I did not want that to be the case.

Two rooms down, across the hall, another man was not sleeping. Jeff, too, was wondering about death and what he would do if his wife suddenly died. He was questioning life, his role within it, and his ability to control what now appeared to be random mortality.

No one else knew about Valerie's death. I was sitting on the floor of a strange hotel in a city where we were never supposed to be, dealing with what no one could have imagined would ever happen. *How will I tell people? How will this affect my children? What do I say to them? I can't bear to think about that. Did we do everything we could in trying to save her? I should have been able to prevent this. Maybe I should have been the one who died. What did Val mean when she said she didn't feel well? Was she trying to tell me something?* My mind cycled back to the beginning and again through its progression of questions. I wanted my old life back, the one I'd had just yesterday.

# Chapter 21

## *Poor Connections*

---

Morning arrived quickly, and though I must have slept, I wasn't sure when. The new day brought a new set of anxieties. I needed to let others know what had happened.

*How should I let people know? When is the best time? Whom should I tell first?* were questions on my mind as Jeff, Jenn and I ate our first meal in thirty-six hours.

"Who do you think you will call first?" Jenn asked.

I looked at her and slowly shook my head. "I don't know, Jenn," I said.

I had a company calling card and, prior to the trip, had looked up the Belize country code, though it would provide little help in southwestern Guatemala. I had a few telephone numbers in my head but needed more.

Jeff discovered the hotel had Internet access, and after waiting for the single computer terminal to become available, we started the search.

I knew the first round of calls needed to start, but whom should I call first? What should I say? What assistance did we need? What help could others realistically provide? I didn't have any answers, nor could we tell them details of how Valerie's body was getting home. We had yet to speak with the embassy staff, and the funeral home would only say that preparations to transfer Val's body were under way. We didn't know when we could leave the country. I wished I had more specifics, but I believed the people I had to call would understand the lack of answers.

I initially thought my parents needed to know, but after more consideration, I realized that meant telling the children. The telephone would not be a suitable way to deliver such horrible news. I needed to do that in person. That task was my duty, and no one else could do it. It would be impossible for my parents to keep the news from their grandkids while they were taking care of them. Even if they didn't say anything specific, the kids would know something bad had happened. I simply could not call my parents.

*Maybe I should call Dan?* Dan was one of my best friends and had been a business partner for many years. He could help coordinate activities in the United States, and I knew his home number and his cell. I would certainly be able to reach him.

*We need a funeral home in the States* was the next item in my mind. I had no idea about funeral homes, other than my recent experience with several in Guatemala. I figured Pastor Jeff knew about that stuff. *I should call him anyway—we could use some words of inspiration.*

I needed to contact Valerie's family. *Oh my God, how can I do that?* They needed to know, but they would have to keep the news from my extended family. I decided to start with Eileen and Steve, Val's sister and brother in-law, as I was sure they could help, and they might know some of the things we would have to arrange once home. *Okay, that's enough people for now,* I thought, as we gathered our belongings from the computer table.

With the "when" and "who" questions answered, the "how" remained. *How do I tell these people Valerie died? What words can I possibly say to them?*

Even after breakfast, my body felt empty. I had a few phone numbers and a general plan—enough to start the process anyway—but I lacked the will to take the next step. With more questions than answers, and not knowing when we could leave the country, the time had come to communicate the tragic news. I went to my hotel room, said a prayer asking for much-needed strength and picked up the phone.

Pastor Jeff was the first person I dialed. It seemed he might know the most regarding possible next steps in the process. Sunday mornings are typically busy times for pastors, and I was sure Pastor Jeff would be busy. I called the general church office number and wasn't surprised when someone other than Pastor Jeff picked up the phone. The voice on the other end of the line was unfamiliar to me, which was good, because I didn't want to discuss the situation with anyone else at the time.

"I know Pastor Jeff was here earlier, but I don't see him around right now. Can I take a message or would you like to call back?"

"Do you know if he went home? Do you have his home number handy?" I asked.

"No, I don't. Sorry. I'm not sure of his home number. Is there something that I can help you with?" stated the friendly voice.

I thanked the person and hung up the phone. *That didn't go as planned.* The unpleasant task, from the very start, was more complex than I'd hoped it would be. I sat on the edge of the bed and considered how no one in my home country had any idea of what had transpired over the past thirty-six hours.

Dan was the next person I dialed.

"Hello, Dan," I said into the receiver. The connection was not clear, and I debated whether I should hang up and start again.

I've often been told I would not make a good poker player, as my mannerisms and voice rarely mask my real feelings, and Dan knew with just those two words that something was very wrong.

"Rod? Hey, Rod, what going on?" Dan asked with concern in his voice.

*How do I begin?*

I took a deep breath and, more matter-of-factly than I intended, said, "Dan, Val has died. We need your help."

"What? Valerie died? Rod, oh my God. What happened?"

The shock and devastation in Dan's voice were unmistakable. He had many questions—anyone would have—and summarizing the sequence of events was difficult to do.

"We're not sure what happened to Val yet. We'll need an autopsy to determine the specific cause of her death. I just really need to get her back home, but we're not entirely sure what that entails yet."

"Where are you now? What can I do? Oh, Rod, I'm so sorry. I can't believe it."

Yes, it was certainly unbelievable, and for many of his questions I didn't have an answer. I gave him my general plan and said I would be contacting a few other people. I also told him I did not yet want my parents and certainly not the kids to know. A true friend, Dan said he'd do anything to help.

Through our brief conversation, I could sense his own sadness building. His voice cracked, and I knew tears were in his eyes. Dan's friendship with Val had grown over the years. He'd gone through some particularly difficult times and had sought Valerie's counsel. Val had a gift in this area, and her comforting and encouraging words had been important to Dan.

"Thanks so much, Dan. I'll be in touch." I slowly placed the receiver on its cradle, tears flooding my eyes and thoughts of Val rushing into my head. I didn't want to think about the conversations yet to come.

The second time I called the general church number, Pastor Jeff was in his office. The connection wasn't very good, but once I had him on the telephone, I didn't want to call back a third time.

"Pastor Jeff, this is Rod Jasmer," I said, knowing my call on a Sunday afternoon was unusual.

"Hello, Rod. How are you doing?" he asked.

"Not particularly well. Pastor, I have some very bad news. Valerie . . . We were on a trip and Valerie . . . Valerie died yesterday."

"I can't hear you very well. Did you say Valerie passed away?"

"Yes."

"Oh, Rod, I'm so very sorry to hear that. Were your children with you? What happened?"

There was unmistakable pain in his voice. Pastor Jeff was a seasoned minister and knew the words to say, but as we spoke, I knew he didn't want to accept my sad words. Pastor Jeff had worked with Valerie often over the years, and like many others I would soon learn about, he had a strong connection with her.

I asked for his help in contacting a local funeral home. Not only did we need a funeral home in the States, we also hoped they could assist us in getting Valerie home. He named a few funeral homes, but this wasn't the time to conduct reviews, so by the time he finished his description of Mattson Funeral Home, I had selected them. I asked if he would explain to them our situation. I also gave him Dan's number and told him I would be calling Valerie's sister Eileen as well. They would likely be contacting him, and he could feel free to discuss anything with them.

By far the most burdensome request I placed on Pastor Jeff was that I wanted to tell my children the news about their mother personally. This was understandable, but it meant not telling anyone. My parents frequently attended our church when they were in town, and they knew several members of the congregation. As a pastor and a father, he understood, and he agreed to tell no one.

I asked him to pray for us. We needed strength, renewal, encouragement and much more, but that was a start.

We said good-byes, and I imagined Pastor Jeff sitting silently in his office, taking in the enormity of the news, his thoughts likely very different from what they had been minutes ago.

I sat on the edge of my bed in Guatemala City and wondered how Valerie's death would affect others within the congregation. A beloved member of the church, Valerie had been active and visible, and her absence would be deeply lamented. For now, Pastor Jeff could only contemplate privately, as he honored his promise to keep the information confidential.

Eileen and Steve had just returned to their house from a weekend at their cabin. As the phone rang, I hoped Steve would be the one to answer. I thought it would be easier to tell him, and for him to tell Eileen that her baby sister had died suddenly and we did not yet know why. When Eileen answered, I could barely speak. She knew who was calling from my first few words and that I was delivering bad news.

"Rod . . . Hello, Rod," was the first thing she said after hearing my voice. "Are you okay? Are you in trouble?"

Yes, by all accounts, we were certainly in trouble, but I wasn't completely sure how to answer. Again, I hoped Steve would just pick up the phone.

Eileen repeated her words. "Rod, what's wrong? Is everything okay?" She would later confide in me how unsettled her feelings were about our trip. There was no other reason I would be calling; something had happened. She first thought of a car accident and wondered if someone had gotten hurt, and then her suspicions moved to a possible kidnapping. None of her suspected reasons for my call were good; however, what I would tell her was beyond anything she'd expected.

"Valerie has died," I replied in one breath, not knowing what else to say. My words, the opposite of sugarcoating a message.

"What?" was her response, much like everyone I'd spoken with so far today. "What?" she said again, though it was clear from the change in her voice that she'd both heard and understood my words. I heard her calling out for Steve to get on the line.

My words, now undeniably etched in her mind, were bad enough to hear once, but none of us realized their answering machine recorded the first few minutes of the conversation. Weeks later, Eileen listened to the message. Hearing the words for a second time was horrifying and heartbreaking. With the push of a button, the message was erased—at least from the machine.

Each conversation held great emotion and made the next call more difficult, but they all needed to be made. By the end of Sunday, April 18, Jenn, Jeff and I were no longer the only Americans who knew of Valerie's death.

Steve and Eileen carried the weight of telling Valerie's other siblings, a short straw I wished on no one. The burden of telling Valerie's mother fell to Valerie's only brother and one of her sisters who lived near their mom. This responsibility should have been mine, but it was more important to share this news with close family by her side. To make a bad situation worse, Valerie's father, the family patriarch, had passed away just four months before in late December. Her youngest child's death just months after losing her husband of fifty-seven years was devastating to Val's mother.

The news of Valerie's death traveled rapidly among her family and friends, even without the tentacles of social media. My hope was that my children would not be among those to hear the message—at least not yet.

# Chapter 22

## *A Promise*

I needed to see Val again. This time I had a specific item I needed to discuss with her. Jeff, Jenn and I believed we could locate the funeral home in daylight and felt the walk might do us some good. The hotel's front desk attendants felt differently and strongly suggested we take a taxi. We eventually decided to heed their advice, and we were glad we had, as it was farther than we'd remembered.

We entered the funeral home and explained who we were and that we wanted to see Valerie. The English-speaking employees who'd assisted us the previous night were gone, and communications became difficult. They called for another person to assist us, and though she seemed to understand our request, something seemed to be bothering her. She stated she would find someone more senior to approve our wishes, which made us suspicious.

She returned and gently told us it would not be possible to see Valerie because they hadn't been expecting us. The exchange was awkward, and the more they said we couldn't see Val's body, the more I wanted to. By the time the third person arrived to assist us, the story changed.

"Yes, of course you can view the body," said the newest person behind the counter. "Just give us a few moments. We will take you to her."

After a short wait, they escorted us to what was more a hallway with a few chairs than a waiting room. The building was much less busy this afternoon than it had been last night. A few minutes later, another woman stated that Valerie was ready.

The area we entered had a metallic look and was certainly not a formal viewing area. The room was relatively large with a brick wall on one side. A plastic retractable curtain, used to partition off an even larger space, enclosed the remaining part of the room. The counters along the stationary wall held equipment and small tools, and the painted gray concrete floor added to the room's industrial feel. Val's body was in the middle of the room on a metal table, similar to, though much wider than, the table she'd spent so much time on at the hospital. A bloodstained yellowed sheet covered her from the neck down, and bloodied rags were present on the table. A red-spattered plastic trash bag, approximately a third full, was on the table next to her leg. The top of the bag was folded over but not sealed. By Valerie's head was what looked like a clear plastic water bottle now three-quarters full with what appeared to be blood. Her face looked like someone had hurriedly applied makeup to it, though her discolored skin and lips were still visible. I touched her face. It felt cool but not cold and rigid.

Touching Val's body instantly distorted my thinking, and a sensation moved up my spine. I shook my head as complete disbelief washed over me. There was no doubt this was Valerie's body, but comprehending the situation was far beyond my ability.

I knew nothing about embalming, and upon seeing the room and its contents, I imagined an infinite number of unpleasant possibilities. Whatever the La Cumbre staff had been doing before we'd interrupted them was evident on the table. Undoubtedly, the blood was hers. I did not want to think what might be in the plastic bag by her feet, and I did not investigate its contents.

The scene was not tranquil, calming or inviting, but none of that mattered to me. I had come to see Val, and this was indeed her body; the items surrounding her were merely extraneous.

There was a particular purpose to my visit. I needed to look directly at her face and tell her I would take care of her children. I would do everything I could to raise them the way she would have.

"I know you loved them so much. I'm not sure if I can do it, and I know I won't be as good as you, but I give you my word I will try." She already knew that I would, of course, but I needed to say it to her.

I meant what I said, but I had no idea how my life would change over the next twelve years. It would be another four years before I would even remember this moment. My instincts would lead me to dramatically alter my life, taking a completely different path, even quitting my career.

I stepped back from Val and moved to the back corner of the makeshift viewing room, allowing Jenn and Jeff to approach her.

"This hardly looks like Val," Jenn said, shaking her head.

"I can't believe I'm looking at her dead body," Jeff replied. "It's like we're part of some sort of dream. I keep expecting her to wake up and smile."

As they looked down at Val's body, the nightmare of the previous day came flooding back, impossible to comprehend. Jenn began to cry.

We decided to walk back to the hotel, now confident we could find our way back and certain we needed to clear our heads. The day was sunny but not as hot as the day before. The walk felt good. We decided to keep walking and find the embassy so we'd know where to go for our appointment the following morning. With the embassy located, we felt confident it would be relatively easy to make our appointment time.

We took in our surroundings and talked as we walked. We didn't have cell phones or radios, and we knew no one. We were somewhere in the southern part of Guatemala, in Central America's largest city, though we had no idea of our specific location. Earlier in the day, we'd asked the hotel staff for a map, but the woman simply shook her head and politely asked if we would like a taxi.

At the hotel, there were more calls and discussions to have. I spoke again with Pastor Jeff, Dan, Steve and Eileen. We updated each other on progress made and exchanged new information. I also spoke with one of the Mattson Funeral Home representatives. They stated they would start the process, though I really didn't know what that meant. Their director, Susan, later provided additional clarity, stating they had already made some contacts stateside and had a call in to the Guatemalan funeral home.

Through all this, Jenn, Jeff and I needed to remind ourselves of the more mundane daily things such as eating, washing clothes and finding bottled water. I had called Continental Airlines earlier about flight options departing Guatemala City, but booking a flight home meant we actually knew how and when Val was getting home. The airline representative said he would be glad to sell me a new ticket and that, at least for now, seats on the flights from Guatemala City to the States were available.

Dr. Carlos remained confident that the work they needed to complete would not delay the overall process. He figured it would take a day or two before all the documents were in order for Valerie's return.

All things considered, Tuesday or Wednesday appeared to be best option for traveling back. We hoped to secure necessary documents from the embassy upon our meeting the next morning that would allow La Cumbre Funeral Home the remaining part of Monday and Tuesday to complete their work. I called the airline again, and I didn't wait long before requesting a supervisor. As I spoke with the airline representative it seemed she was more interested in the situation itself than selling a ticket. I did learn there were no available seats for the Tuesday or Wednesday departures and a limited number of seats for Monday, Thursday and Friday flights. Standby was an option, though given the number of people traveling, she didn't recommend an unguaranteed ticket.

"I just need to get home. Book the latest flight you can for Monday," I finally said.

When I wasn't making calls from the hotel room, I found a relatively secluded location on the second floor overlooking a portion of the city. After the latest round of calls, I needed some air and migrated back to the now-familiar spot. Though my timing was serendipitous, I nevertheless found myself sitting in silence, watching my first sunset without Valerie.

I watched and wondered. *It just doesn't seem real. How could such a thing happen?* If this could happen, anything could happen, and I wondered what might happen next. What would this truly mean for the kids and me? Certainly, a large part of ourselves was gone. Did losing Val mean losing the very essence of who I was? I was still alive, but in several ways, I wasn't sure.

I was on a balcony in a strange hotel in some big city watching a sunset. Val should have been there. She would have liked this. I wished beyond any expectation for many things that evening.

Jeff, Jenn and I found a place to eat nearby called La Estancia. As we ate dinner, we talked about everything we'd witnessed over the past few days and tried to process and comprehend its meaning.

"I knew Valerie was gone after seeing her on the floor of the bungalow," Jeff said. "I'm not sure how to describe it, but when I looked at Val's face, I saw death."

I could tell this was not something he was comfortable expressing, as he hadn't said anything previously. I had no real idea what he was talking about, and I asked him to explain what he could.

"I just knew. I'm a bit of a war history buff, and I've read about battlefield casualties describing the 'look of death' in detail. They say you can see death before it happens. The image was unexpected, but I believe I saw it," Jeff said.

The confession brought with it a powerful sensation. I thought back and tried to remember the look on Valerie's face as she lay on the floor in Tikal. I had not seen what Jeff saw. Maybe I didn't know what to look for. Maybe I'd chosen to ignore it.

# Chapter 23

## The Embassy and La Cumbre

Our hotel was unlike any hotel I'd known. There were no elementary-aged children running around the hallways, no preteens swimming in the pool, and only a few business types preparing for their meetings. The hotel catered to families excitedly waiting for their final adoption paperwork. For all intents and purposes, it was a transfer terminal, a place where lives came together, where families formed. My situation wasn't quite the same.

Here in this "pinnacle of happiness," I faced the first random person who innocently asked me how I was doing. He likely expected me to say, "It's going terrific. I'm great," or at a minimum, "Just fine." I couldn't bring myself to say any of those words. For a second, I thought of telling a sliver of my story, but nothing came out of my mouth. I simply nodded and left the room.

Later in the day, another happy but anxious man asked me, "Are you and your wife adopting as well?" I froze and just looked at his face. I was standing in a small semicircular protrusion of the hotel and was unable to simply turn and leave without stepping toward the man. I struggled for a suitable reply. *I should just say no and move on. Should I say we are not adopting, as we already have three children at home? I could say my wife is here—well, she's not really here . . .*

"My wife died yesterday," suddenly poured from my mouth. The combination of words was odd to say and likely more unexpected to hear. The man's excited expression was gone. Neither of us knew what to say next. We departed in opposite directions.

~∽∾∽~

We wanted to be among the first to arrive at the embassy in the morning. Our instructions, as specifically communicated by Ms. Clair, were to go to the far side door of the embassy, as the line would likely be long at the main entrance. Ms. Clair would not be at the embassy that day, but she assured us we should have no problems. Once inside, we were to say we had an appointment with Ms. Sophie, the head of United States Citizen Services.

Walking toward the embassy, we were feeling good that we'd indeed eluded the crowds as no one was in line at the front entrance. We rounded the corner of the building and there, at our secret side entrance, was a line of people stretching three-quarters the length of the building. Our feeling of specialness vanished quickly.

"We must not be the only ones who have a meeting with Ms. Sophie today," Jeff said.

We took our place at the back, and after a short time, we became antsy to see if our appointment with Ms. Sophie would carry any weight. It did and successfully moved us to the front of the queue. Once through security, we entered a large room already filled with people. We eventually spoke with an embassy employee, and after we again used the Ms. Sophie appointment technique, he directed us to a smaller room with fewer than a dozen people waiting.

The appointment angle had proved useful, and we felt fortunate we weren't still standing in line outside. When they called our number, the three of us proceeded to the bulletproof glass window.

"Yes, we have an appointment with Ms. Sophie," I said, looking at the young woman on the other side of the thick glass.

"Ms. Sophie is not available at the moment, but I can certainly help you," said the woman.

Though I was prepared to start the conversation, Jenn wasn't so sure. She'd set up the meeting with Ms. Sophie through Ms. Clair and wasn't going to concede so easily.

"We have a scheduled meeting with Ms. Sophie and would like to speak with her, please," Jenn said politely but firmly to the woman. The woman behind the glass didn't deviate from her position, insisting she could help us.

We explained why we were standing in front of her, and she listened sympathetically. After providing what we thought was a sufficient accounting of the details, we stopped speaking.

"So, how can I help you?" she asked.

*We just recounted our traumatic ordeal and why we are here in front of you.* I thought they would have specific instructions for us. I guess I was expecting something more.

After a slight pause, Jenn and I started doling out questions.

"We need to know what to do to take Valerie's body back to the States. What documentation, besides what we have, do we need? I assume we need more paperwork; can you get us what we need? Do you know anything about La Cumbre Funeral Home? Are they a reputable company? We don't have a death certificate—do we need something like that? How do we get one?" Those were the first questions we threw at her.

Before she could respond, I asked, "I'm scheduled to depart later today—can my friends finalize the remaining requirements if I leave?"

"Hmm . . . okay. I believe I understand now. Please hold on, and I will be right back," she said, walking away. When she returned, she had questions for us. We answered each of them, but before we could ask any of our own, she left again. This time we watched where she went and surmised the person she was talking with was her supervisor, coaching her on how to handle our request.

Upon her return a second time, the woman said, "I will need you to write a power-of-attorney letter authorizing your friends to act on your behalf in order for you to leave the country."

"This is necessary for Valerie's body to be transported back to the States?" I asked.

"Yes," the woman answered.

"What should it say?" Jenn asked.

"Well, it is a legal document that will give someone—say,

Jennifer here—the right to act on your behalf," she continued.

"Yes, I know what a power-of-attorney letter does, but what part of our situation are we talking about?" I asked.

"Just be general in stating your situation. It doesn't need to be long. There's a chair over there, and when you're finished, don't take another number, just bring it to me. Next number please," said the woman to the people gathered in the room.

The request to execute a power-of-attorney document seemed strange, though we convinced ourselves we needed to write it. Specifically how the document should read and how it could get Valerie's body home wasn't clear, but if the piece of paper solved our dilemma, so be it. With little choice, we began drafting the letter.

We moved to the end of the room and collectively drafted a power-of-attorney letter. We produced the simple one-page handwritten document on a piece of white photocopy paper provided by the embassy.

It read:

> *I, Rod Jasmer, give permission and authorization to Jennifer [last name] to handle all matters relating to my wife, Valerie Jasmer, who died suddenly and unexpectedly on Saturday morning,*
> *April 17, 2004.*

We gave it a final read-through and determined the document was as complete as it would get. We waited a short time for our embassy assistant and then handed her the piece of paper.

"Does this work for your needs?" I asked.

"Okay, this looks like a good start. Let's add a date and a

place for your signature, Rodney. I'll also add a statement to the bottom." She took the paper, added a date and my name with a line above it, and a statement reading: "Subscribed and sworn to me on April 19, 2004." She then added another signature line below the newly written statement and suddenly stopped. The woman, now looking toward the ceiling, started tapping her pen on the paper. "This document should probably be written in Spanish. It's the Guatemalan officials who will need to read it," she said.

Jeff reiterated what he thought he'd just heard, "The letter needs to be in Spanish."

"I'm not sure we can do that," I said.

For the next few minutes, we actually discussed creating a Spanish version of the document. Jeff was the most accomplished in the Spanish language, so it would fall on his shoulders to attempt the feat. Soon the idea of it became absurd, and we stopped abruptly.

"You're asking us to draft a legal document in a foreign language. I can barely speak the language much less write it. I'm sorry, but that seems ridiculous. Is this really necessary to get Valerie home?" I asked.

"We would like to speak directly with Ms. Sophie now," Jenn said matter-of-factly through the small hole in the thick glass. "We had a personal meeting set up with her, and we want to have that meeting." The assistant made another visit to the back of the room and soon another woman approached the window.

"Can I help you?" said the older woman. Her presence and mannerisms suggested she'd heard a few stories over the years.

"We had a meeting scheduled with a Ms. Sophie this morning," I said.

"Yes, we would like to speak with her directly," Jenn added.

"I'm Ms. Sophie. How can I help you?" said the woman. We started to interact, and her gruff exterior faded. Within fifteen minutes, she'd answered many of our questions.

"Let me make a few calls. Please have a seat, and I'll be back shortly," she said, disappearing into the interior of the room. Roughly twenty minutes later, Ms. Sophie approached the window, her assistant close behind.

"I have spoken with Dr. Carlos, and we are missing an important piece of paperwork from the hospital. The funeral home is working to correct the issue, and they feel confident the document can be obtained relatively quickly," Ms. Sophie stated to us.

"What missing paperwork?" was the obvious question I asked.

"We already have the doctor's signature, and we provided it to La Cumbre. We have a copy. Here it is," Jenn said, digging through the pile of papers we'd brought with us.

"Yes, I am aware of that document. However, there is additional information required before the body can leave the country. Dr. Carlos can tell you about it when you see him."

The more questions we asked, the more we thought of, and Ms. Sophie knew the answers to most of them. She assured us I could leave the county without waiting for the additional paperwork and that they would work with La Cumbre to complete the process.

"What about the power-of-attorney document? We have the one we drafted in English but not the one we need in Spanish," I said to Ms. Sophie but looked at the younger woman standing behind her.

"You can forget about that; neither document will be necessary," she said, moving on to other items.

They requested Val's passport, which I was glad to have received back from Edmundo. Ms. Sophie's assistant took it to the back, and by the time we finished our discussion, she returned the passport with holes punched through all the pages. They also provided us several copies of Department of State Form 180, titled "Report of Death of an American Citizen Abroad."

"I made you several originals of this document, as you will likely need them once you are back in the States. They will come in handy," Ms. Sophie said.

I didn't really know what that meant but nodded. Just before we left, Ms. Sophie said, "Remember, Dr. Carlos is expecting you at the funeral home and would like to speak with you."

We thanked her and started retracing our steps out of the building, past the line of people slowly moving in the opposite direction. I wondered if any of them had a meeting scheduled with Ms. Sophie.

<hr />

We made our way back once again to La Cumbre Funeral Home and finally met the man we'd spoken with many times on the phone. Dr. Carlos took us into his private well-furnished office and seemed to be very understanding of our situation. He first apologized profusely regarding viewing Valerie's body the day before. He stated this was a terrible mistake on their part, and they should never have let us view her in that location, in that condition. I, on the other hand, thanked him for letting me view her on a Sunday and asked him to pass along my gratitude to his staff as well. We got the impression several individuals had received strong reprimands regarding the matter.

I asked Dr. Carlos about the partially filled plastic bottle that was next to Val yesterday. Dr. Carlos confirmed the bottle indeed contained Valerie's blood and would accompany the body back to America for the autopsy. He went on to state that La Cumbre did an excellent job of embalming and considered itself one of the best in the country, yet he added that their work might not be the same as American standards. His words seemed sincere but troubling nevertheless. We got the impression he was in a hurry to get Valerie's body transferred to the States. I was glad our interests aligned.

In a sort of self-analyzing monologue, Dr. Carlos started to explain his life and losses, including the loss of his child. He explained the similarity between our situations, using his wife as an example of how she struggled with the loss of their child and how the loss of a child is much worse than that of losing a spouse. The message was difficult to follow. If this was an attempt to make me feel better, it wasn't working, and we were all anxious to move on in the conversation.

We went through the additional paperwork, and as politely as he could, Dr. Carlos asked for additional payment. Regarding the timing of Val's departure, Dr. Carlos reluctantly told us there was one little problem. Though a Santa Elena doctor and the local official had signed release documents regarding Val's death, they hadn't signed a specific government release form required for the body to leave the country. He explained that an e-mail or a fax version would not be sufficient; it needed to be an original. Obtaining it would be relatively easy in many places of the world but not here. The choice was either an unreliable and relatively expensive flight or a full day's drive— roughly seventeen hours round-trip— between the two areas.

We asked how such an important document hadn't been discovered missing until now. However, Dr. Carlos seemed not to want to dwell on the matter. He simply stated several times to trust him to get the paperwork as soon as possible. After the answers started to sound the same, we moved on in the conversation.

The funeral home's strategy regarding Valerie's departure was under way. Any further input and options from us appeared limited. We had little choice but to trust they would come through, relying on the perception that they wanted to transfer Valerie's body as much as we did.

"When can we plan on Valerie's return?" I asked.

"We are scheduling for tomorrow morning. Final paperwork should be here tonight. If not, the next day at the latest," said Dr. Carlos.

Dr. Carlos said my hometown funeral home had been in contact with them, and that it completed another require-ment—ensuring Valerie's body had a specific destination once she was back in America.

It appeared any influence I had on the process was now nonexistent. I could leave the country. Jenn and Jeff would remain in Guatemala to handle whatever else was required to ensure the shipment of Val's body to the States, presumably within a few days.

Before leaving La Cumbre Funeral Home for the last time, we wanted to see Valerie again. Dr. Carlos made a call and told us he would have the body moved into a proper viewing room. Within ten minutes, we were ushered upstairs. We now had a familiarity with the large La Cumbre complex, though we were no more comfortable with it.

This time, the funeral home staff was clearly prepared for our visit. Valerie's body was on a table in the middle of the room covered with a clean cloth. Long red velvet curtains surrounded the room, and soft pile carpeting covered the floor. Every element of this room was in stark contrast to the metal and concrete of the last viewing. The bloodstained rags surrounding Val's body were gone, flowers replaced the spattered plastic bag at her feet, a water bottle filled with her blood no longer sat by her head.

Valerie's surroundings had changed and so had her appearance. They had pushed most of her hair to the side of her face, and the rest was now in bangs hanging just above her eyes. Bright-red lipstick covered her lips, and red cheek rouge dominated her face. If someone hadn't known Val well, they would not have recognized her. Even to me, she didn't look like herself. At least not the way she'd looked just a few days earlier.

Saying good-bye, though I knew this was only Valerie's earthly body, was not easy. I was leaving my wife in Central America and returning home without her. I couldn't have done that without Jeff and Jenn remaining in the city. There was more I needed to do, things I couldn't take care of from a hotel room in Guatemala.

# PART V

*A Solemn Return*

# Chapter 24

## *Not Quite Home*

---

Arranging my return flight for Monday, April 19, turned out to be a good call. Dr. Carlos had provided a driver to drop me off at the airport and bring Jeff and Jenn back to our local headquarters, the La Casa Grande Hotel. For the first time, it seemed like splitting up was the right thing to do. Jeff and Jenn would stay in Guatemala in case any additional problems arose while I returned to begin the solemn task of sharing the bad news face-to-face. Dr. Carlos stated there might be additional arrangements necessary, though he didn't specify any details. His comment surprised no one.

The line at the Guatemala City International Airport's Continental counter stretched nearly out the front door, and I cannot remember a time when I was more thankful to be a frequent flyer. Within fifteen minutes, I'd checked our two travel packs, received a boarding pass, and headed to customs and the security check.

The anxiety of passing through these checkpoints, particularly in a foreign airport, magnified the events of the past couple of days. I felt uncomfortably alone without the security and reassurance of my travel partners. I interacted with a mass of people who had no idea what had happened. They had their own lives and were dealing with their own feelings, oblivious to what had happened to Valerie. Answering even the simplest of questions, looking into people's eyes, was beyond enervating.

*Don't you know what happened? Didn't you read or hear about the foreign female tourist who died in the country? Do you know that my wife isn't coming home with me?* They did not. I was the lone person in this sea of people who knew. The feelings amplified my isolation. I wanted more than ever to be home.

I'd cried on and off over the past few days, but I was done for a while. My disbelief, however, grew stronger. I found myself constantly hanging my head and slowly shaking it. *I can't believe this happened. How could this have happened?* My legs moved me forward from muscle memory with little participation from the rest of my body. I kept looking around me as I moved through the terminal. I wasn't sure what I was looking for, but I didn't see Valerie's face in the crowd of people. I knew seeing her at the handbag kiosks was impossible, but I looked nevertheless.

My mind never left Val, what had happened, or the burdens yet to come. I eventually made it to the gate and sat in the remotest seat I could find.

I was about to get on a plane and return to America without my wife, my best friend. Without Valerie. The thought kept circling in my mind. Everything we had seen and done together in our nineteen-year relationship was over. There would be no more. It no longer felt like my own life.

The driver dropped Jenn and Jeff back at the hotel, and after a light meal, they set out to find the travel agent Dr. Carlos had suggested. Continental was not as understanding with them as they'd been with me, despite their efforts to explain the circumstances. They would need to get creative in booking their flight back to the States. While watching the travel agent type at his computer, they suddenly heard a familiar voice behind them. Ms. Sophie from the embassy pulled up a chair directly behind them.

"I stopped by the hotel, and they told me you were over here," said Ms. Sophie. "I have some additional documents for you."

Jenn and Jeff were elated. "Thank you so much for all your work," Jenn said. They had some trepidation in making their return flight arrangements without having complete assurance Val could return. Now that feeling was gone. They too could make flight reservations and leave this place and maybe a few of its unpleasant memories behind.

I trudged onto the plane and took my seat. I reached into my backpack and removed the Continental-issued earphones they had furnished on the flight to Belize and plugged them into the armrest. Personal music selection is now second nature to many people with hundreds and even thousands of songs at our disposal at any given time. In 2004, digital music was not as common. I had not listened to music since Val's death, and even though I had no control over the playlist, it seemed the lyrics spoke personally to me. Each song seemed to make more sense than anything else surrounding me. In my state of mind, I could find a link to my life in every song that played.

I wasn't sure if my strong desire to connect each event and make sense from the chaos came from my scientific training or simply who I am, but I wanted to line up all the pieces and understand each one's meaning. I began thinking back to comments made by Dr. Carlos during our last meeting. He had been concerned about my well-being and discussed his own experience with loss. He had described his feelings and those of his wife, their struggles of loss, and how difficult their ordeal was for them. He said his wife believed it would be easier if she were no longer around, and she toiled with wanting to live versus wanting to die. The thought kept running through my mind. I could not imagine losing a child, but I was starting to understand the feeling of losing a spouse.

I could understand the desire to join the departed, as it might indeed be easier than living. But I had three children at home. As much as they needed both of us in their lives, that was no longer an option. My kids would need a parent more than ever, and I needed them.

Yes, I would have gladly exchanged places with Val. At the hospital, I'd wished I had been one under the sheet. But that was not how matters stood, and I tried not to think about what my life would be like in the future. I needed to somehow deal with this reality. I'd made the promise to Val and would not back away from it. I needed to see our kids through whatever came next, be with them and take care of them. I felt a need to get my body, as well as my mind, in shape.

The desire to write and capture the moment came over me. I wanted to talk about Val and let people know the type of person she'd become. There would be a funeral at some point—I knew little about such things—but it would be a good time to tell others about Valerie. I wasn't sure if I could do it justice, but I needed to try.

Ink began to flow onto the paper I'd found in my backpack, and I made notes on her life, our lives together and our kids.

*The kids. What do I say to them? How can I possibly tell them? Oh my God, I just can't bear to think about it.* I began to shake.

*I get back so late,* I said to myself. *I guess it will be another late night.*

Making my way through the terminal in Houston, I began to feel a rising anger. Frustration and aggravation had certainly been part of my mood over the past few days, but now I was gripped by concentrated anger. With each step, I felt more and more indignant. By the time I reached the customs line, I was enraged and unsure what to do about it. The line was not particularly long, but I cursed it.

When my turn came to approach the agent who was sitting in his chest-high cubed station, I took a deep breath and reminded myself that the customs agent knew nothing about Valerie's death.

"Did you have a nice time on your travels? Do you have anything to declare?" asked the middle-aged man as he looked at my passport.

"No," was out of my mouth so forcefully it startled me. I was tired, certainly, but there was much more to my one-word answer than that. Something buried deep within me had yet to reveal itself. In retrospect, I had kept this angst buried far too long.

The agent looked up from his tasks and opened his mouth but said nothing. As I prepared to explain my abrupt answer, he motioned me through the line, neither of us saying another word.

I was thankful to be moving again, thankful no other words were necessary, thankful to be back on American soil.

The short layover in Houston gave me a chance to locate a row of pay telephones and continue to plan. Eileen and Steve confirmed that they would drive to my house in the morning from Madison. They were bringing their daughter, Nicole, nineteen years old at the time, for additional support. The kids loved Nicole, so it seemed like a great idea.

Dan and I decided it would be best if I stayed the night at his house after my late arrival from the Minneapolis/St. Paul Airport, effectively postponing telling my folks and the kids until the next morning. Some rest and a slight deferment seemed like a good plan, as I still had no idea how I would tell the kids.

My body moved mechanically, but my brain was in a fog muddling thoughts together. I knew my life was not over, but it was altered beyond imagination. It seemed unrealistic to contemplate what direction my life would take, let alone the lives of three others.

Driving to Dan's, I noticed my surroundings were in stark contrast to the conditions of just a few days ago. I had experienced culture shock before, but nothing like this. I wondered how many hospitals I'd already passed. I pictured clean rooms, outside entrances with doors, glass windows covering openings in the walls, shelves fully stocked with supplies. I thought about how quickly an ambulance would respond with well-trained paramedics and first-class equipment. Air rescue was one phone call away. All of this had been far beyond my reach a few days ago, but here it's taken for granted.

Just before ten, I walked up the steps to Dan and Pam's house to find them waiting in the doorway. We hugged and cried, comforting one another. Pastor Jeff soon arrived as well, and we settled into the living room. It felt good to be among comforting friends.

The conversation eventually turned to the obvious.

"Do you mind telling us a little more of what happened?" Pastor Jeff asked, Dan and Pam nodding.

I began slowly, not really knowing where to start or how much detail to share. This was the first time I told parts of the story to others. I began to describe the events that had happened over the previous few days, and as I did, my mind became clear. Specific details came quickly to mind, though I described only a few key elements. I don't remember stopping to ask if they understood or if they had questions. The words flew from my mouth. Soon it was after midnight. I had energy again, and no one was eager to leave.

Pastor Jeff and Dan looked at each other and shook their heads. If they hadn't heard the account directly from me, it would have been hard to believe. They were also concerned about my state of mind.

"Rod really needed to do some emotional venting," Pastor Jeff said when I was out of the room. "The words and feelings just needed to come out."

"He's not his typical self, but I don't sense he's out of control," Dan replied.

"I agree. That was something I was specifically looking for," said Pastor Jeff.

We could have talked even longer, but it was already late, and we all needed some sleep. The next day would bring a new set of challenges. After prolonged "good nights," Pastor Jeff left, Dan and Pam went to bed, and I took my travel pack into another bedroom. It had felt good to talk with friends and be together, but just as quickly I was again alone, something I was about to experience for a long time.

~~~

Just after eleven Monday night, the phone rang in Jeff and Jenn's room at La Casa Grande Hotel.

"There's someone here to see you," the front desk manager said to Jeff. By the time they got out of bed, there was a knock on their door. A representative from La Cumbre Funeral Home had a package for them. They now had a copy of all the documents necessary to transport Valerie's body out of the country. Jeff signed for the package, and the last piece of a complex Guatemalan puzzle was now in place. Valerie would go home the next day.

# Chapter 25

## *Facing a Formidable Day*

---

Several scenarios played out in my mind, but I decided to let the kids go through their normal morning routine of waking up, getting dressed, eating breakfast, and running down the driveway just in time for the school bus. For them, the day started out like any other.

I believed it would be too much of a shock for my parents if I showed up unexpectedly, so I called them, letting them know I was back from the trip and would see them soon. This made sense at the time, but in retrospect, I'm not sure this was the best idea. My parents knew something was wrong, and the extra half hour of waiting for me was agonizing for them.

"Hello, Jasmers'," came the familiar voice of my mother when she answered the phone.

I froze. I knew what I wanted to say, but the only thing in my mind was Valerie had died, and I couldn't say that. The news of Valerie's death would shatter their world. I needed to stay calm, at least on the phone.

"Hi, this is Rod," I said. Then without hesitating, I continued. "I'm back in the States, at Dan's house. I'm driving home now and will see you soon," I said, trying not to say too much but letting them know I would be showing up six days ahead of schedule.

"What's going on? What happened?" was my mother's response.

"I'll see you soon," I said.

The brief conversation was heart-wrenching. I said good-bye again and hung up the phone.

I thanked Dan and Pam and started the final leg of my journey home.

*What do I say to them?* I repeatedly thought during the drive. The two people I was driving to see would not suspect the words coming from my mouth, but I could not think of a way to soften the blow. I did not want to think about the anguish I was about to release on my parents. My parents loved Val dearly, as another child, really—the daughter they'd never had. Their wills specifically listed Valerie as a member of the family. I knew they would be devastated.

Each mile only increased my dread. Prior to this point, the people I had told face-to-face had not been close friends or relatives, but that was about to change.

The minivan barely hit the driveway before my folks came out of the house and entered the open garage. By the time I got out of the car, my parents were standing in front of me.

They knew something was very wrong, but they had no idea just how wrong.

"Why are you back so soon? What happened?" were the first words from my mother's mouth. I reached my arms around them and, without any preface, said, "Valerie died." The words were clear and unmistakable, yet unable to be fully processed.

"What?"

"Valerie died suddenly on our trip," I said with a quivering but clear voice.

"No. Oh, no . . ." said my dad as he raised his right hand to his mouth. He began to shake, and as the horror reached his entire body, his legs collapsed beneath him. He fell to his knees on the asphalt driveway. We helped him to a chair, and my mother and I simply held each other and cried.

I grew up Missouri Synod Lutheran, by no means an outwardly expressive religious denomination. Our family attended church regularly, and we prayed before each meal, but having my father ask us to join hands in prayer was not an everyday occurrence. We had never prayed as a family so courageously or so completely in my life as we did then. We prayed for many things, among them strength to get through this and particularly for my children.

I had prayed off and on over the past few days, even asking Pastor Jeff to lead a prayer on the phone. I needed help and strength to get through the next few weeks. I looked for answers but also questioned why God would allow something so awful to happen.

Steve, Eileen and their daughter Nicole pulled up in my driveway within an hour after I arrived. Just hearing their car drive up and envisioning their sorrowful faces sent my emotions churning.

I'd cried many times before, but seeing family for the first time evoked an even deeper response. We embraced and cried as never before. Val and I had spent a significant amount of time with them. They were family, they were friends, and I loved them dearly.

"Your dad doesn't look very well," Eileen said as we moved into another room. It was true—he didn't look like himself. Even after several hours, he had difficulty standing and even speaking. Steve said the raw emotion and utter devastation upon my father's face would stick with him forever.

My beloved wife was gone, but others had lost a significant and cherished person in their lives as well. We did not concern ourselves with what would come next; her death itself was what we grieved.

But the kids. The kids had no idea what news was heading their way. They remained comforted in the belief they would reunite with their mother in less than a week's time, unaware of the life-altering news. The day had already been hard. That task and its resulting feelings weighed heavily on me.

I decided it would be best if I told them at their schools, arranging for a private meeting area without their friends and teachers around. I did not think my parents, Steve, Eileen or even I could pick them up from school without them knowing something very wrong had happened. I also didn't want to wait the entire day for them to come home and then give them the bad news. To me, things tend to be more traumatic at night, and at least we would have the day to console one another. If news of Valerie's death started to move through the community, I certainly didn't want it to reach my kids. Right or wrong, the plan was set.

I called Linwood Elementary School, where Erica and Peter attended, and explained that we would need to speak with the kids and the reason. Most of the teachers and administrative staff knew Valerie personally, as she was a regular volunteer at the small school. Though stunned and heartbroken, they were very accommodating, offering to help in any way they could.

We decided Steve and Nicole would go with me to the school to support both the kids and me.

*How do I do this? What do I say? Oh my God, their mother is dead. I don't want to do this.*

I decided to start with Peter. Sweet Peter, only in the second grade—his big heart easily captured the affections of many. Peter and Valerie were the ones who showed outward emotion most easily. Meeting people and making friends were easy for Peter, and he was thoughtful with others. He and his mother had enjoyed a great bond. At eight years old, what would he be able to comprehend, and how would he handle it? I wondered how this would affect him.

I somehow knew, even at his young age, that Peter would understand the depth of this loss. I had no doubt that even with the passage of time, he would remember his mother well and the times they'd spent together. This was what I needed to cling to, as it supplied a small amount of inspiration to make the dreaded task a little more bearable.

Ms. Carlson, the school counselor, suggested her office. When we were ready, she would call Peter from his classroom. I would never be ready, but it was time. I closed my eyes and tried to slow my heart from pounding and my mind from racing. I again wondered, *What could I say? How should I act? What would make this news better?*

Unexpectedly, other thoughts flashed into my mind. *It should be me they are talking about. Val should be the one alive. She should be the one consoling the kids. Of course she would do a much better job than I.* This would not be the last time I wished I had been the one to die. Thinking about Valerie speaking to the kids about my death, I realized I would not wish that moment on anyone, certainly not Valerie. I was the one sitting in the school office waiting for my child, and in a profound way, not wanting this responsibility cast upon anyone else gave me courage to face the small boy now entering the room.

His eyes brightened as he saw me out of pure excitement to see his dad.

"Peter," was the first word from my mouth, void of enthusiasm, full of sorrow.

Even though Peter was a young child, he noticed the inflection in my voice, which quickly removed the feeling of a joyous reunion. As he made his way toward me, his face was already changing, puzzled. I'm sure he wondered why dad was at school. Why Mom and Dad were back so soon from their trip. Why Uncle Steve and Nikki were there. I could see it building in Peter within the three seconds it took him to reach my arms. He sensed something must be wrong. His worried look told me I could not put this off any longer.

I took Peter in my arms and gave him a solid hug.

"Peter, Mom died," I said, the words coming out of my mouth more quickly than expected. "I'm so very sorry, Peter."

For an instant, Peter said nothing. I could feel his arms tighten and then squeeze around my shoulders as he processed the words, trying to get closer to me. He started to cry, and so did the rest of us.

"Peter, your mother loved you so very much." I told him we all loved him so much.

After a few minutes, I could think of nothing else to say. I searched my mind. There had to be something else I could say, something encouraging or comforting. Nothing entered my mind, and I said nothing else.

Peter asked no questions. He had heard my words and understood exactly what they meant. We continued to hug each other and cry. Eventually Peter released his grip around me, and he sat on my knee. His face was almost more than I could bear. His expression showed defeat and panic and fear. I again reached my arm around him, telling him how much I loved him.

We probably could have stayed together in that small office the entire morning. After some time, everyone stood, but I didn't know if I could trust my legs. Their instability and the energy it took to move were odd sensations.

I told Peter I needed to tell his sister Erica the sad news. Nicole and Peter went to the principal's office next door, and Steve and I prepared ourselves for the next round. I still had two more small hearts to break.

There was no doubt Erica had a best friend in the world, and that was Valerie. Erica had school friends and relatives her age, but none were as close to her as her mother had been. To find them cuddled up together on a chair, the couch or the floor was commonplace, and I heard, "Where's Mom?" from Erica several times a day. Mom was her security and happiness in a big, impersonal world.

Erica often saw the world in black and white, with little room for gray areas. I wondered how she would react and process what she was about to hear. A significant part of her comfort, strength, and daily support would suddenly be gone. I knew she would feel the immediate pain, as her essential supporter would never be there again. I wondered what other effect this would have on her. Those thoughts were for another time, as I needed to get through this first step of altering a little girl's life.

*Maybe I was too direct with Peter. Do I need to be subtler with Erica?*

"Erica, you're going home now," said Ms. Gulbransen, Erica's fifth-grade teacher. Erica was in the library that hour, and the news of going home early puzzled her, but she was too shy to question one of her teachers. They went back to Erica's main classroom and got her backpack and a few books. It seemed strange to Erica that the teacher was taking her to the office, but if Grandma was getting her out of school early, it really didn't matter.

Erica's reaction to seeing me was similar to her brother's. At first there was a burst of joy. But her delighted smile soon became a look of confusion and then of uncertainty, sensing that something was wrong. I once again reached out and held my child, wishing the embrace was the only thing required.

I hesitated slightly, and with her in my embrace, I said, "Erica, Mom died on our trip."

My words were devastating. How does an eleven-year-old girl put such horrendous words in context in her mind? The answer was directly in front of me as her small body lost its rigidity and dissolved into mine. I could not get close enough to her nor her to me. I wanted to wrap her in my arms, rescue her from the suffering and refill her with the love she was undoubtedly feeling was now lost.

"Erica, I love you so much," I said.

Erica just nodded, tears streaming down her face.

"We all love you—especially Mom. She was always so proud of you."

These words were easy to say, as they were true. I did not say things would be fine or that everything would be okay. Maybe I should have, but I didn't know if they really would be.

The fifth-grade child sitting on my lap knew her life had just changed forever, and like me, she had a fear of the unknown.

A few months earlier Erica had written a letter to her mother for a Thanksgiving project.

It read:

*Dear Mom,*

*I am thankful for you because you are very loving. Also because you take me to lots of places that I have never been to or saw before. You show me how to do all kinds of different things like how to plant flowers or how to set up something. You like to play games with me but I am always going to win. You take me shopping and buy me stuff. You are very funny like the time when you were shaking the puppy chow and it fell all over me. Whenever I am talking you listen and look at me. You also take care of me and you are very helpful like if I have homework you help me.*

*And that is why I am thankful for you.*

*Love,*

*Erica*

Children who write letters to their parents, even for a school project, typically show a genuine honesty. The short note reflected the characteristics of their relationship. I had no doubt Erica was indeed thankful for her mother's presence in her life.

As with Peter, moving was hard to do. I told Erica that we had already told Peter, and he was with Nicole in the next room. Erica's body and her mind now conflicted, her knees buckled as she exited the room and grabbed the counter to support her weight. Erica saw Nicole and Peter coming out of the adjacent room, and she rushed to Nicole's side, using her cousin to support her body.

We said our good-byes to the staff at Linwood Elementary. They shared their sympathy, saying they would watch Erica and Peter closely, and asked if there was anything else they could do. We thanked them for their understanding and support. We headed home, crying and doing the best we could to console one another.

I soon became anxious once again. I wanted to stay with Erica and Peter, but still had to call Alisha's middle school. This call was not as personable or as easy as it had been with the elementary school—not offensive, just not as comforting.

Hanging up the phone, I could think of little else but telling yet another child her mother had died. Though already completed twice that day, the task still elicited a sickening feeling in me.

I wondered if anything could make the impact of the news any easier for Alisha. It bothered me I had told my other children of their mother's love in past tense. Their mother *loves* them, not just *had loved* them, and she *is* proud of them, not *was* proud. The thoughts added to my internal struggle.

As the oldest child, Alisha would understand more clearly what the loss of her mother would mean to her life. A thirteen-year-old girl needs a mother, and Alisha had carved out a special niche for her mom. Val talked about how treating each child fairly didn't mean equally, and Alisha's time with Mom was different from her siblings'. Though Alisha was a young teenager, I couldn't remember her and Val arguing. They understood each other, though their thoughts were likely very different.

The surroundings were different at this school, and I found myself wishing we were back at the elementary school. Steve, Nicole and I took a seat in a small room within the office and let the administrator know we were ready to see Alisha.

The office assistant entered Mr. Forssmann's geography class and asked Alisha to come with her to the office. Being called to the office in the middle of the day was unusual, and I'm sure Alisha suspected that she was in trouble for something.

Seeing me in the office was equally strange. The bright smile on her face quickly fled as she tried to imagine what was going on. She looked at me and then at Steve and Nicole, and I knew she could see misery in our faces.

"Hello, Alisha," I said, trying my best to keep a steady voice.

"Hi. What are you doing here?" she said with great wonder. "Where's Mom?"

*I wish your mother was here to see you. You look more grown up now than I remember you were only a couple of days ago. You look so much like her. I so wish I could answer your question differently.*

I wrapped my arms around my daughter as the words that her wonderful mother had died crossed my lips. It was as hard to get out this time as it had been with the other children. I managed to drain the blood from yet another little face, crush a beautiful smile, replace curious eyes with fear and tears.

# Chapter 26

## Understanding the Meaning of Words

I discovered children react very differently than adults when faced with difficult situations. The striking distinction was consistent in each instance.

Though all the adults I told about Valerie's passing had greatly differing personalities, the resulting dialogue was similar.

"I thought you were on vacation."

"Is everything okay?"

"What's wrong?"

"Are you in trouble?"

"What?"

"What . . .?"

"Oh my God."

"I can't believe it."

"How did . . . how could . . . why did . . . this happen?"

The way I shared the news in most cases was clear and concise: "Valerie died." They all heard and understood the words, yet what the mind heard did not translate into belief. There must be a misunderstanding, an incorrect connection. "Valerie" and "died" did not compute. The implication was too difficult to grasp, much less accept. I know too well the feeling of not wanting to accept it.

The children did not ask any of these questions. They heard the same words, but they did not need to hear them again. What, where and how were only details to them, and they couldn't care less about the answers. Their father had just told them that their mother had died. That was enough to hear; no additional clarification was requested. They needed simply to be held, to cry and to hold their mother's love in their minds.

Jeff and Jenn remained at the La Casa Grande Hotel. Word had spread to other guests that someone staying at the hotel had lost his wife and that his friends were still at the hotel. Most people would smile or politely nod at Jeff and Jenn, not knowing what to say.

The hotel's uniqueness meant steady streams of new relationships forming in front of them. Huddled around a newly adopted child, each family's happiness was unmistakable. Perhaps the stress of recent events influenced their thoughts, but the scenes of joyful adoptions removed any doubts Jeff and Jenn had on the subject. Upon returning home, Jenn and Jeff would begin their own adoption process

After telling my children, we could finally share the tragic news with others. Social media today would have made this easier, but that wasn't an option in 2004. We began telling those closest to us, knowing others would learn in due time. Within hours, the phone started to ring, e-mails hit my inbox, and one by one, shock, grief and offers to help our family poured in.

For those staying at my house, this was the first day of grieving; for a few others, the second. For me, it had been so many days already, and I was miserable and despondent. I began to question every decision I'd ever made.

# Chapter 27

## *Sangria*

---

From the very beginning of the incident in Tikal, time moved quickly. Except for the drive to Guatemala City, my life seemed to hurtle through each day without hesitation. If someone had asked me if I thought time would slow to an agonizing pace or speed up so that I couldn't catch my breath, I would have guessed the former. I would have been wrong.

A completely new set of activities now ensued. Various arrangements and transportation to and from the airport, hotels, my house, church and the funeral home needed to be planned. People brought their campers to our house in order to lodge more people, and others opened their homes to out-of-town friends and relatives. As quickly as it had started, it seemed departure arrangements were under way.

I helped as I could but was limited to only a few minutes here and there for any given task. The days were a constant flow as each activity streamed into the next. I wanted to go away, to think, to be alone, to make some sense of everything, but that would have to wait.

More than anything, I wanted to know what had happened to Valerie. Even as Dr. Carlos had strongly encouraged me not to have an autopsy completed in Guatemala, I wanted the answer. I also wanted to know if my children were in any danger from any hereditary condition.

Susan, the director of Mattson Funeral Home, became a real ally, advising us on many things and helping to select the University of Minnesota hospital system to conduct what they called a private autopsy. There was one catch. They required an up-front payment to perform the service if Val wasn't part of the Fairview hospital system. Not wanting to bother me with details, Susan and Eileen arranged for the procedure, not knowing that Val was indeed part of their system. The up-front payment for their services was eerily similar to the fee requested to secure air transport in Guatemala. I guess not everything was different in my home country, particularly when it involved money.

On Tuesday morning, April 20, workers at La Cumbre Funeral home sealed the unique locking mechanism of a white casket containing Val's body. They surrounded the metal casket with cardboard and enclosed it in a wooden crate for the journey to the States.

With the papers in order, there was no need for boarding passes, security lines or delays at the airport. Val's official title was now "cargo." All 584.2 pounds were loaded underneath the passengers' section of Delta flight 280. With a plane change in Atlanta, Val's body would arrive at the Minneapolis/St. Paul Airport at 8:21 p.m.

Just after Valerie's body was unloaded, Susan was at the cargo area filling out paperwork for transport to the next destination. Mattson Funeral Home staff could have picked up the casket, but with her husband (who also worked for the funeral home), Susan personally handled Val's delivery. The wooden braces, cardboard and metal-framed casket just fit in the cargo van for the forty-two-mile journey to the funeral home.

It is customary for the funeral home director to view the body once in his or her care, and given the circumstances, Susan was particularly interested in making sure everything was in order. They removed the outer layers of the crate and cardboard boxes to reveal a simple off-white casket with several scrapes, dents and rusted hinges.

"Interesting choice," Susan said. "Not too many people select a casket like this. It certainly is a special-order piece here." A casket making a journey from Central America would most likely be a bit banged up. "Curious though—the outer container didn't look this beaten up," Susan said, suspiciously.

The outside of the metal casket paled in comparison to what Susan saw inside the box. The material on the inside looked like it had at one time been white, but the fabric was badly faded and stained with a yellowed tinge in places. There appeared to be splattered watermarks in several locations.

"Did they get a used casket?" Susan said to her husband. "Rod didn't say anything about this. Would anyone ever use a casket more than once? This is completely unsuitable."

Susan had never met Valerie or seen a photo, but from what she'd heard, the body in the casket was much different from her mental image of Valerie.

"I think the family needs to see this," Susan said. "I'll call them in the morning prior to the autopsy. We also need to ask if they were considering an open casket at the funeral."

Jeff's alarm sounded at 3:40 a.m. on Wednesday morning, and he and Jenn were finally going home.

"It feels weird to be leaving. Part of me doesn't want to," Jeff said.

"I know what you mean. I feel like we're leaving Valerie behind—like her spirit is still here," Jenn replied. At the same time, they didn't want to stay. They'd been through a lot during their short time in the country, and they wanted to be home.

"My condolences once again. I'm sorry about what happened to you and your friend," offered the clerk as they checked out. The kind, simple gesture made an impact at 4:45 in the morning.

"Would you like to view Valerie's body before we go to the university for the autopsy?" Susan asked on Wednesday morning.

"Yes, of course," I said, sensing a slight uncertainty in her voice. "Is everything okay?"

"Well, it's just that . . . it was a long trip. I'm not sure she looks like what you are expecting."

"Not what I was expecting? I'm not sure what that means."

"If you could bring some photos along, that would be helpful for me to get perspective on the way she looked."

"I'll bring some along. We have lots of photos." I wondered why Susan needed photos with Valerie's body right there in front of her.

"We can also go over details for the funeral," Susan said, sounding glad we were coming to the funeral home.

Steve and Eileen had yet to see Val's body, and they asked if they could come along. I welcomed their presence and was grateful for their help and support.

Susan and her assistant prepared for our viewing, and seeing the casket again made Susan shake her head. "I just don't understand," she said, as much to herself as to her assistant. They opened the casket and continued the inspection from the previous night. Val's hair was styled awkwardly around her head, and the generous amounts of lipstick and makeup were even more striking this morning.

"What's that bottle doing there?" Susan's assistant asked, pointing toward Valerie's left side. Wedged in the crook of her arm was what resembled a plastic water bottle. Susan carefully removed and examined it. The object was most certainly a disposable water bottle, roughly three-quarters full of a dark substance. Susan gently shook the bottle, confirming to herself that the container held some sort of liquid. Affixed to the side of the bottle was a strip of masking tape with the handwritten word SANGRÍA.

"Why would they include a drink in the casket with the body?" Susan said.

"Maybe it's a Guatemalan custom," Susan's assistant said.

"I was just in Mexico and drank sangria. I don't know why they would put some with the body. Maybe this was Valerie's favorite drink?" Susan said, trying to come up with a plausible explanation.

As they thought of other theories regarding why a wine concoction would be added to the casket, they began to examine the bottle more closely. By tipping the bottle on its side and lightly shaking it, a portion of the liquid would splash against the clear plastic and cling to the sides, forming a noticeable film around the inside of the bottle. The mass of liquid was dark, almost black, but the thin portion of liquid clinging to the bottle's neck appeared a much brighter red. It was much thicker than the sangria Susan had consumed on vacation.

Susan suddenly became uneasy and placed the bottle back into the casket, questioning her previous conclusion. "I need to check on something," Susan said to her assistant as she hurried to her office. Sitting down in front of her computer, she typed the letters s-a-n-g-r-i-a into the first English/Spanish conversion website she found. The words "Blood, Bleeding, Bloodletting," appeared on her computer screen. Though shocking, they weren't completely unexpected.

# Chapter 28

## *Inconsequential Selections*

E ileen, Steve, and I arrived to a warm welcome from
Susan. She showed us to a conference room, and after
we'd exchanged pleasantries, Susan respectfully shared
information regarding other countries' approaches to embalming,
makeup, and presentation.

"Many other countries—and I would certainly include
Guatemala in this group—prepare a body much differently
than we do. Most people here are not accustomed to this,"
Susan said. She seemed to be telling us everything was okay
while at the same time letting us know Valerie might not look
quite right to us. "Even I was a little shocked when I first saw
her," Susan said. "I haven't done anything to the casket or to
Valerie at this point. I wanted you to see it for yourself."

Having not seen Valerie's body in several days, I found myself wanting to view her body again. I walked into the viewing area by myself; Steve and Eileen offered me some time to be alone with her. Susan was correct in her assessment—Val's body did not look exactly like herself—thought not that dissimilar to how she'd looked at La Cumbre. Her lips, face, and neck were puffed considerably, and her stomach and arms seemed to be sunken into her body. I'd known Val for almost twenty years and had never seen her with this hairstyle, the bright-red lipstick, or the highly noticeable red cheeks.

For the most part, her superficial presentation didn't particularly bother me, as Valerie's body was back home. The long ordeal of getting her here flashed in my mind, and I was so grateful for everyone who had helped along the way.

Steve and Eileen's reaction upon seeing Valerie's body for the first time was not quite the same as mine. Only twelve days earlier, Steve and Eileen had seen a vibrant woman, alive with spirit. Even though they were now expecting the worst, they did not like what they saw lying in a beat-up, discolored, stained coffin. This was not Valerie. At best, it was a poorly painted corpse vaguely resembling their sister. This was no longer the person they'd known their entire lives. They didn't want to remember her this way, or for others to see her like this.

We moved into the conference room and Susan proceeded to discuss, as kindly as she could, that the condition of Val's body and the casket were completely unsuitable for most people. She didn't want to insult us or make us think she was trying to sell us another casket, but she needed to share her concerns.

Susan and Eileen were sensitive to the conditions in which I'd made choices, and they gently asked me to consider the way

Val would likely want things to happen and suggested redoing a few things. I understood the points made and agreed that others might not understand her current state or the limited options that had been available to us at the time.

As the funeral planning discussion continued, I became distracted. I could hear the conversation, but only as distant noise. My mind wandered back to when things had changed. Details of our current discussions didn't matter; they were merely consequences of a tragic and unpredictable circumstance.

Valerie died in the jungle of a Third World country and was placed awkwardly in an old plywood box too small for her body, crudely secured with an unprotected lid with a worn hammer and previously used nails. Her body had been subjected to hour upon hour of excessive heat and constant motion on a horrendous journey involving several different modes of transportation. People helped us along the way, doing what they could, giving her what they had and giving of themselves. The details of the funeral decisions before me felt irrelevant.

With a twitch, my attention snapped back to the funeral home conference room. "Okay, yes. Let's get whatever you think we need," I said, with no idea of the particular subject they were currently discussing.

"One final thing—are you thinking about an open casket?" Susan asked as Eileen gauged my reaction. I had no immediate response, so Susan continued.

"After the embalming chemicals set, you can no longer make large alterations to the body, particularly the face and neck. I'm not sure how much I can do to modify her appearance."

I knew that people were accustomed to seeing Val a certain

way, and I wondered if her current condition was the last impression I wanted them to have of Valerie. I was equally as sure that many people at the funeral would like to see her, and maybe a few needed to say something directly to her, as I had.

"We need an open casket. I want people to see her." I was hopeful Susan could help to make Val's body look more like herself, but regardless, I wanted to allow others to see her one last time. I'm not sure everyone agreed with my statement.

Susan said they would do their best and she would personally oversee the presentation. After a pause, she again looked at me and said reassuringly, "This will work out fine."

I wasn't sure if she was simply agreeing with my wishes, but Susan's words made me feel more confident about the decision.

It seemed fitting that the fourth and final casket Valerie would need was made of wood. We lived in the forest with trees surrounding our home. Equally fitting was a casket of the same material as the wooden box we'd initially placed Val's body in. I kept this second reason to myself.

All the plans now revolved around the autopsy, and the people conducting the examination wouldn't give a precise time frame for its completion. Many people needed to make travel and flight arrangements, so we went ahead and set up the visitation for Sunday and the funeral for Monday.

On Thursday morning, Susan transported Valerie to the University of Minnesota medical examiner's office. Unsure what to do with Valerie before the autopsy, Susan simply removed Val's clothing and placed her in a hospital-type gown. Not wanting to change anything else, she left the makeup intact and the bottle of "sangria" in the casket.

Later that same day, Susan received a call from a representative of the medical examiner's office stating the autopsy was complete and Valerie's body was ready for pickup. Though a variety of tests remained, they had what they needed to complete the examination.

Susan signed the papers and returned Valerie to the funeral home. Later that evening, she bathed Valerie's body and removed the makeup placed there three and a half days ago. Susan could now see Valerie in a new light. She would indeed make Valerie's body presentable in the coming three days.

〜✺〜

Friends and relatives provided comfort and well wishes throughout the next few days. I truly appreciated their concern and the time they spent with my family and me.

During a meeting with Pastor Jeff about the visitation and funeral, our associate pastor stopped me in the hallway and said, "I don't know anything else to say to you, Rod. This is a huge loss."

I nodded. If a pastor had run out of things to say, then so had I.

Decisions about music, singers, Scriptures, pallbearers, readers, eulogies and so on needed to be made, and resolutions seemed hard to come by. "Have you given any thought as to where you would like Valerie's body buried?" Pastor Jeff asked, switching topics.

"No, I haven't. I have a choice of cemeteries?" Who knew there were options when it came to cemeteries? Maybe everyone except me. I was tired of options and making decisions. Though, as I look back, this was only the beginning of endless decision-making. Most of the things we were deciding on seemed exceedingly immaterial. Valerie was dead. Now what would my family do? How would my children grow up without a mother? These were the concerns that weighed on me.

Pastor Jeff could tell I'd become more stressed since we'd met in Dan's living room. "Rod, how are you doing? You seem overwhelmed. Are you okay?" he asked.

"Yes, yes, I'm fine," I replied, much too quickly, giving it no thought.

Our church's cemetery, located in another part of town, didn't offer the calming feeling I was hoping for, nor did our local township cemetery just up the road from my house. The less-than-cordial and blunt township staff didn't sit well with Valerie's relatives.

"Have you ever heard of the Henry Ernest Cemetery?" Susan asked in a late-afternoon call. "I didn't want to bring it up right away as it's a little out of the way. It certainly isn't for everyone, but it's quiet. I think you may like it."

From the very first moment we turned off the narrow tar road onto the washboard dirt road, still a half mile from the cemetery, I liked it. Trees and state-owned undeveloped land surrounded the area. The setting was tremendous. Though farther away from our house, it was worth the drive.

Three of Valerie's sisters and I met with Elliot, the new sexton for the cemetery. Shortly after our meeting began, he told us we could select any location we liked for Valerie's final resting place. We took that mission seriously and ultimately decided on a spot far away from others, near a group of pine trees. It seemed a little unusual that we could pick any location within the cemetery's boundaries, and we questioned Elliot about it.

"Well, with that location, you sure won't need to worry about anyone being close to you. In over a hundred years, we've used less than half our space. It will be another hundred years before we are out there," Elliot said.

I wanted to say a few words about Val at the funeral. What, specifically, I wasn't sure. I wanted something meaningful and from the heart, and I needed some time to organize my thoughts.

My shed, which was forty-seven steps from my house, became the place where I found refuge. The notes I'd begun on the airplane were helpful, but I needed to build other words around them. There was much to say, and no matter what I wrote, it didn't seem adequate to describe my feelings or Val's incredible life.

Distractions of the house and its inhabitants were nonexistent in the shed. It was quiet, and I could clear my mind and write my eulogy. Instead of writing, however, I found myself repeating the story in my head. "Why did this happen?" I repeated out loud. "What went wrong? What did I do wrong? The kids can't be without her. I would do anything, *anything*, to have her back." Through my tears, the words on the screen blurred.

One evening, with several people in my living room, someone asked about what had happened. Once asked, many others seemed to want to hear the story. It would be the second time I'd shared any of it with others, and it was as strange to tell this time as it had been during the first. Minutes turned to hours as I unwound the story. I elaborated on some details and skipped others altogether. Some would ask a question or two, but for the most part the group simply listened in silence. Over the years, this pattern would repeat itself many times.

My daughter Alisha appeared at the edge of the stairs and peeked around the corner of the living room. She joined in and listened for a while, then backed out when she'd heard enough. She was older and more curious about the details than either Erica or Peter, but she did not want to hear too much at once.

Answering questions about the incident was never a burden or exceptionally difficult for me. It would bring up powerful emotions, and I would reexamine my actions each time, but I understood why people would ask. I would likely have had similar questions. The discussion allowed me to consider clues regarding the death itself. Had I missed something I should have seen? Talking about Valerie, strange as it might seem, was comforting, as during the discussions it seemed she was still part of our lives. The conversations confirmed for me that I needed to write these words down and capture the moments forever. My kids would appreciate the full story when they were older, and it would be another way to keep Valerie's memory alive.

"Remember to call Elliot back," Eileen said. "He just called again while you were in the shed."

"I forgot to call him. I'll call him right now," I responded.

"Hi, Rod," said the voice on the other end of the line. "I'm afraid I have some bad news. I was completely wrong in stating you could select any location in the cemetery. The location you selected to bury Valerie's body will not work."

"Are you kidding me, Elliot?" I asked, knowing he was certainly not kidding.

"No. Sorry. That part of the cemetery hasn't been surveyed, and the board won't let you use the spot you selected. I feel so bad. I knew that was a perfect location for you, and I told you it was okay."

*I should have known this would happen,* I thought, having previously questioned the location. "What does this mean? You know we weren't excited about many of the other spots."

"I know. I have two other locations I believe you'll like. They're in the central part of the cemetery, in the oldest section."

"I'm not sure I follow you. How did these spaces suddenly become available?"

"We can't locate the original owners, and their annual five-dollar maintenance fee hasn't been paid for many years. Rod, you should look at these. They're in a really nice spot, located on higher ground, near a tree."

"Elliot, but what if—" I stopped my question and revised my thinking. "Okay, that sounds fine. I know the general location you're referring to. I don't need to see it. I'll take both of them." With a solution to the situation, it wasn't worth questioning it further.

As Pastor Jeff had thought, Val's passing affected many in the congregation and was a wake-up call for many members. A large demographic at St. Paul Lutheran was between thirty-five to forty-five years old, involved in various activities and raising young children. Valerie had been a vibrant barely forty-year-old woman with three children, running a large segment of the youth program, and she epitomized our church at that time. Such an unexpected loss was difficult on many levels, including the sudden realization of one's own mortality. Many people could see themselves in Val and wondered if something like this would happen to them and how they would cope.

A member of the church said to me, "If such a tragedy could happen to Valerie, it could happen to anyone. It could happen to me." This same sentiment resonated with many people, and its reach extended far beyond our church.

Alisha, Erica and Peter had not seen their mom since she'd said good-bye to them nine days ago. I wasn't sure they wanted to or needed to see her body now, but on Sunday, they would be standing in a room full of people, and their mother's body would be there. Seeing their mom in a casket would be traumatic, and I thought it might be best if we went to see her as a family with no one else around.

On Saturday afternoon, we went to the funeral home, and though several others came along, we entered the viewing room as a family of four. I could only imagine what they were thinking as they saw their mother's body in a half-opened box. The startling sight brought tremendous emotions, fears and uncertainty about what this all meant for their future. Once again, a vast sense of loss washed over me.

I'm not sure whether the decision to view Valerie's body with my children prior to the visitation was good or bad. In discussing the event with them now, they believe the experience wasn't any better or worse than the other events surrounding their mother's death.

The visitation was set for 3:00 to 7:00 p.m. on Sunday afternoon. We arrived fifteen minutes early to find the large room already filled with people. Valerie, in her new light-oak coffin and with subtly applied makeup, lay silently and, it seemed, much more peacefully, against the far wall. Stacks of smartly crafted memorial pamphlets were on a small table in the entryway, and photos of Val and our travels filled much of the room. Flowers and plants decorated the remaining areas. I could hardly believe my eyes.

I wondered if the arrangements were real or if the funeral home set these flowers and plants out for everyone. As I examined the displays, the personal notes attached to each suggested they were indeed from caring people who also loved Valerie.

I'd had direct influence over many events during the previous few days, and as barriers presented themselves, we'd overcome them. This setting was beyond my control, though, and had taken on a life of its own. I glanced toward Valerie, as I would instinctively do in many situations, looking for guidance, for safety and companionship, insight and encouragement. I was out of my element.

"What do I do now?" I asked Eileen. My instincts, which I'd come to rely on for guiding me through recent events, were fading. As the room filled with people, I felt alone and lost. The kindness, compassion and sympathy were overwhelming. I saw people I'd known all my life, others who were part of a distant past, some entwined in my current life, and still others I had never seen before. All standing in a line, they moved toward me, paying their respects to Valerie, offering their deepest sympathy to my family and me, each in their own way. The experience was powerful and time flew by. I thought two hours must have passed, but for some reason when I checked my watch, it showed 7:34.

# Chapter 29

## Driving Away

Before I knew it, the next day had arrived, and I was getting ready to attend my wife's funeral. Peter wore a new suit bought by his godfather, Ron. Purchasing his first suit wasn't something my eight-year-old wanted to do. The reason he needed one in the first place was because his mother had died, and Peter wanted nothing to do with it. In the store, his emotions overcame him, and he erupted into a full-blown fit. He didn't want to try on clothes, much less wear a suit to what the grown-ups called a funeral, whatever that meant. Trying to ease the moment, Ron told him he could burn all the new clothes if he wanted to after the funeral.

"I can burn these clothes up after this is done?" Peter asked. "Okay, you promised," he said to Ron as he slid his arm into the new jacket.

The girls' funeral clothes, purchased during a much-needed break from the house with their aunts, made them look beautiful and so much like their mother. Plenty of people were around to ensure such details were attended to. Watching others help my children with even these simple tasks showed me how little I knew of all the things Valerie had done for them.

Looking at my selection of ties in the bedroom closet, I ached over how young my children were and how much support they would need. I started to shake my head, wondering how I could ever replace Valerie's presence in our lives and that none of the ties seemed appropriate for my best friend's funeral. I felt my mood shifting. Next to my ties were Valerie's clothes. In fact, most of the clothes, shoes and belts in the closet were hers. I stared at her stuff, resentment building inside me. Her clothes hung there, mocking me.

I suddenly reached out and grabbed as many of her things as I could and began pulling them from their hangers. As I did, I caught her scent in the clothes pressed between my arms and face; I stopped, dropped the clothes, and cried. Regaining my composure after a short time, I once again stood and looked at my ties. *Get it together, Rod,* I thought, wondering how I would react at the funeral surrounded by so many people.

Driving to the funeral, I thought of the episode in my bedroom and realized some feelings needed to come out—better alone in my bedroom than in front of hundreds of people. I also realized that maybe I wasn't nearly as strong as I'd thought. I questioned my ability to run my own life, much less help the children with theirs.

The church quickly filled to capacity, which surprised no one. Susan showed us a small drawer inside the casket that we could place items in if we wanted to. Each of the kids had made a card for their mother, and I'd written a note to her as well. Just before the service, the four of us gathered and stared at Val. We each have vivid memories of this moment, though we cannot recall if we exchanged any words. I opened the drawer, and we placed our last mementos near her body. We had viewed Valerie's body for the last time.

I felt the need to show strength and kept my head up, not really understanding why. It was a feeling I hadn't felt before. I wondered if I was trying to be brave, or if I was trying to show the kids we would make it through this ordeal.

In the sanctuary, I saw many people I knew and some I couldn't recall ever seeing before. Flowers adorning the front of the church made it look like a funeral, but someone else's, not Valerie's. After Valerie's death, I'd viewed her body several times, changed her clothes, and placed her into the first coffin. Perhaps that had helped me become more comfortable seeing her this way. I knew they would soon close the casket, never to be opened again. The finality of the moment pierced me, and I felt an absolute hollowness.

The funeral offered closeness, an opportunity for people to express their feelings and share their personal experiences with Valerie, whether out loud or to themselves.

My part at the lectern seemed relatively easy; talking about Val always seemed effortless. I shared how we met, our friendship and a few of our adventures, then thanked everyone for their gracious support. Nothing needed to be more complicated than that.

I sat back down and wrapped my arms around my children. In front of us and slightly to the left was a large covering of red roses on what people commented was a beautiful oak casket. To me, it was merely another wooden box.

Even at the conclusion, it did not feel like my wife's funeral. Our friend Ron recorded the ceremony, and though I have never viewed the video, I wonder if it would seem as foreign now as it did then.

The weather was typical for mid-April in Minnesota. The temperature hovered in the mid-fifties, though a north wind and clouds made it seem much colder. The little cemetery was full of vehicles, the temporary shelter alongside the burial site was full, and many people stood wherever they could find a spot.

The interment service at the cemetery was more real than the funeral. There was a sense of peace at this site. This is also where I failed to do something that I should have done.

I did not wait to see the casket lowered into the ground, the vault closed and the first shovels of soil placed into the hole. I was thinking of the people at the church waiting to have a meal, the ones at my house wanting to see me before they left, and the people at the cemetery needing a ride. I could have planned things differently. I knew Valerie's burial would take place upon our departure, and I should've been there.

The remorse hit me as I drove away. I had left Valerie's body on top of the partially frozen ground. We had gone through so much to get her here: overcome overwhelming obstacles, managed countless complications and hindrances, wrestled with emotions, made decisions—right or wrong—and we'd pushed on. I had not completed this final act in our long journey. The omission carries great weight with me, and to this day, I regret not completing the task.

# PART VI

*Simple Words*

# Chapter 30

## Understanding the How

With the funeral and all its associated activities behind us, family and friends began to depart. Their families had needs as well.

I had little idea of how to proceed along my new path, but those thoughts would have to wait. My yearning for closure to Valerie's death continued to heighten. I'd asked Ludovic and Julie during our ambulance ride, and again at the hospital, what they hypothesized might have caused Val's condition. Given her age, her general physical fitness, and no visible external causes, they'd suspected a brain aneurysm but emphasized that it was only speculation. This theory certainly seemed plausible to me, but it wasn't enough. I was determined to move from speculation to knowing precisely.

The Department of State, Form Number 180, Report of Death of an American Citizen Abroad states "cardiorespiratory arrest, cerebral rupture aneurysm." We believed this information came from one of the documents provided to the embassy staff, most likely from the nearly unintelligible writings of a Guatemalan doctor we never recalled meeting. Jeff, Jenn and I cannot remember anyone besides Ludovic, Julie, the initial hospital attendant, and the coroner examining Val. We suspect the doctor's notes and interpretation of Val's death came from other hospital staff or interactions with Ludovic and Julie.

Maybe the search for definitive answers was the scientist in me, or just a husband looking for answers, but I wanted details. Were there warning signs we missed? Was it symptomatic of her environment? Could we have done something differently to save her life? Was it hereditary? These and many more questions ran rampant through my mind.

I had no doubt the medical examiners would pinpoint the exact cause of Valerie's death. We see it on television and in movies, and read about it in the newspaper. A team of specialists exhumes a body from the ground years after death, and the autopsy routinely indicates a precise cause. I was sure there was a solution to this puzzle.

Susan gave me the name of the person she'd dealt with to set up the autopsy, and within a few days after the funeral, I called to discuss the procedure. The medical examiner I spoke with stated several people were involved in the examination and the interpretation of the results. This was positive news as I assumed that the more people looking into the cause of Valerie's death, the better.

I wanted the examination team to know Valerie's background, information about our trip, and the fact that she had children. I wanted to make sure they understood how important the results were not only for closure but also to evaluate if my children were at risk of a similar affliction. The person stated they appreciated the information and would consider all of it in their findings. This reinforced my optimism that an ultimate cause would be determined.

In subsequent conversations, I provided them with a description of Val's recurring nightmares, curious if there was a link between them and her death. To my surprise, one of the doctors said there might be a connection, though another member of the team disagreed, stating he didn't believe the two things correlated. The differing responses were reminiscent of what we'd dealt with from the very beginning in Guatemala.

During my phone inquiries, the examiners stated the preliminary autopsy results suggested the cause of death was not a brain aneurism as originally suspected. The new information led to further questions, but that was all they were willing to provide. I would need to wait until the final report.

The autopsy report arrived in a standard manila envelope on Friday, May 7, 2004. I was both anxious and nervous. I now held a document that would tell me specifically how and why Valerie died.

The head of autopsy services had signed the cover letter attached to the report, and it included his direct phone number and his condolences regarding the loss of my wife. I wasn't expecting that level of sincerity or such a personal, thoughtful letter, and it took me by surprise. He also mentioned it was highly unusual to send such a report to a nonmedical individual, as they typically sent it to the attending physician. The letter didn't state the cause of Valerie's death.

I flipped it over to begin reading the attached report. The first paragraph talked about the incident itself and the actions carried out while trying to save her life.

*This paragraph is just a summary of what I told them.*

The report then provided an overview of her cardiovascular, respiratory, and gastrointestinal systems, which I breezed through quickly looking for the concluding remarks. As I turned the next page, my eyes immediately moved to the section titled Summary and Interpretations.

My pulse quickened, and I could feel my hands perspire. I read the words much more carefully now, not wanting to miss any of their specific meaning. Words like possible flap-valve effect, old ischemic changes, and sarcoidal granulomas appeared not to play a role in the patient's death.

*So what* did *play a role? Where's the conclusion?* The information had to be in the report somewhere.

I reviewed the next three-and-a-half pages, which included much smaller print and bore the title "Clinical." The section described minute details of internal organs, tissues and their interconnected systems. And then the report simply ended.

Where was the conclusion? What was the reason Valerie died? My initial nervousness faded to disappointment. I knew little more now than I had before opening the autopsy report. I must have missed something. I hurriedly turned to the front of the document and went through it a second time, wondering if they could have forgotten the page that clearly stated why Valerie had died. Though I didn't understand all the medical terminology, the words I most wanted to read seemed to be missing. The second time through revealed no more information than the first.

I'd spoken with other members of the medical examination team, but not with the person who'd signed the autopsy report. We'd previously learned that this doctor was a nationally recognized medical expert, so I was confident that if I could speak with him directly, he would be able to answer my questions.

We finally connected the following week.

"Hello, Rod. Yes, I remember this case. Valerie, wasn't it? I'm so sorry about your loss," said the medical doctor and professor of pathology.

I thanked him for his concern and started asking questions, specifically mentioning that I couldn't locate any conclusive remarks regarding Val's death.

"It can be so tragic for someone as young as your wife to die," the doctor continued. "It is my understanding she had no obvious medical conditions prior to her death. Is that correct?"

"Correct. I've thought about that over and over and cannot think of anything that was off either prior to or during the trip." I again thanked him for his concern, though I wanted facts, specific answers, details—not sympathy. As I pressed him more and more, he began to get my point.

"We're not completely sure of the root cause of death," the doctor said. "We know her death resulted from a sudden loss of blood to the heart. Why, we can only speculate."

"Please give me your best speculation then."

He explained they'd discovered her left and right coronary arteries, which supply oxygen-rich blood to the heart muscle, came off the aorta anomalously high in comparison to normal

arteries. In particular, her left main coronary artery came
off the aorta at a very acute angle of fifteen degrees (versus
a normal ninety-degree angle). This severe angle might have
constricted blood flow. If the area failed, essentially pinching
off the artery, there would be a sudden loss of blood to the
heart. The results would be catastrophic.

These were the technical findings of the autopsy: they had
ruled out a brain aneurism, stroke, or a heart attack caused
by artery disease. We discussed if our hiking or the altitude
had anything to do with Valerie's death, and though any given
environmental condition might have contributed, he could not
say for sure if any one thing precipitated her death. I asked
about my children and any possible hereditary concerns for
them. Again, he was very understanding and sympathetic to
my questions; however, he suggested I speak with our family
doctor about these concerns.

His words carried with them an uncertainty, and I felt
a heaviness in my body. I understood, but I did not want
to believe what the doctor said. I always trusted we would
eventually know the exact cause of Val's death. I didn't want
lingering questions or ambiguity. Now a noted expert in the
field of determining death was consoling me and telling me he
wasn't sure what had happened to my wife. I felt disappointed
and let down.

*I can't believe I may never know definitively what caused
Valerie's death.* The thought was hard to contemplate, and I
couldn't wrap my head around it.

A few weeks later, I received additional autopsy results
from their analysis of the brain. Everything was normal, and
it provided no further clues to the mystery. The finalization of

the autopsy provided an opportunity for additional analysis by other people. Eileen and Steve's contacts in the medical field provided volumes of written material discussing theories and various other possibilities. Concern for my children's well-being became the focus. Ultimately, the consensus from the medical community was that Valerie's condition was not familial and therefore not a medical concern for my children.

My yearning for a specific answer to Val's passing would take years to overcome. Theories alone will need to suffice. The bottom line is no one on earth knows for sure.

I was eager to see our family doctor and ask him directly about some of the thoughts I'd been having.

"Doc, if this would have happened in the States, say, at my house, would the outcome have been any different?" I asked.

"That's a difficult question to answer," he replied. "From what you've told me, and from what I've read in the autopsy report, my opinion is no. I do not believe so."

He went on to say it would take time to get an ambulance to my house, which is approximately twelve miles from the hospital, and neither the ambulance nor the hospital might have had the resources necessary to immediately alleviate Val's condition. Transportation to a larger hospital likely would've been required, further delaying treatment.

"In cases like this, Rod, there is little we can do to save a life. It is similar to an athlete who collapses without warning. I believe Valerie wouldn't have made it even if she'd been here."

I wondered if his response was merely for my comfort or if it was actually a fact-based conclusion.

"Now let's talk about you. You really don't look very well. Have you been sleeping?"

# Chapter 31

## In the Recesses of the Mind

A troublesome thought still wrestled with my peace of mind. It had first emerged while we were changing Valerie's clothes in the hospital.

"Valerie's hope didn't come true," I had said to Jeff and Jenn as we awkwardly tried to get Val's arm into a new shirt.

"What's that?" Jeff said.

"Remember what Val said . . . uh, nothing. Forget it," I had replied, suddenly embarrassed that I'd brought up the subject and then wondering if the message I recalled was even real or if I'd made it up in my head.

My mind would frequently try to recall what I believed was a particularly unnerving set of words written in an e-mail. After the funeral, the desire to view the message grew as the days passed. I retreated once again to my makeshift sanctuary in the shed and turned on my computer. I was eager to open the e-mail that Jeff had sent to selected friends and family members prior to our trip, yet apprehensive about reading the actual words it contained. I'd previously read the document, but the specific words—I just needed to be sure.

My eyes acutely focused and my lips involuntarily forming each word, my mind slowly processed the e-mail's contents. The words lingered both mentally and somehow physically, as if someone else were revealing them to me.

> *– Original Message –*
> *From: Jeff*
> *Sent: Thursday, March 25, 2004 8:39 AM*
> *Subject: To Belize*
>
> *. . . we will be traveling with the Jasmers who are anxious to hit the road again after having three kids. Val's primary goal on this trip is to come back alive . . . I'll report back when (if) we come back.*

Many people have uttered similar words prior to an adventurous trip. Val was a young, seemingly healthy woman, with no signs of impending trouble. She would have told me if anything had been bothering her. Then again, without realizing it at the time, she had.

The simple sentence conveyed in Jeff's e-mail, coupled with Valerie's words of "I don't think we should go," said mere hours before our departure, had become much more significant with the passing of a few days.

Valerie had not achieved her goal.

Making sense of chaos, putting order to random events and reasoning why things were the way they were became my life well after the incident passed. Thousands of senses, memories, decisions, thoughts and feelings—I wanted them all to add up to one thing, one answer, one mystery solved, peace and closure.

But they didn't add up to one thing. They can't, because what happened didn't make sense. Just because I wanted to construct logical organization out of tremendous confusion, it didn't mean the pieces would, or even should, fit together.

Only now do I appreciate my relationship with Valerie for what it was, without trying to find further meaning in what happened. Though it was all too brief, I simply need to accept and value the time we spent together. Like the chaotic collection of tiny blinking lights that suddenly appeared around us from the sea of fireflies, I will try to enjoy and embrace experiences in my life, exclusive of wondering why. Sometimes we're given moments in our lives that are simply beautiful, brilliant and meaningful—without explanation.

# Postscript

On Monday morning, April 26, 2004, the day of Valerie's funeral, Jenn had a doctor's appointment. "Jennifer, you're pregnant," said her family physician. It seemed impossible! Jenn and Jeff had tried for years to have children. They had recently made the decision at the La Casa Grande Hotel in Guatemala to start the adoption process.

"Val would be so happy," was how Jenn told me, and I knew she was right.

"You scaled the gates at the hospital, ran from angry guard dogs, completely passed out on the Santa Elena hospital floor, and you were pregnant that whole time?" I asked, astonished.

Jenn and Jeff could hardly believe it themselves, but in December, Jenn gave birth to a healthy baby boy. As a dedication to Valerie, Jeff and Jenn used the name Joseph for his middle name. Valerie's middle name was Jo'an, sometimes called Jo. I would learn some years later that others had also named a child in honor of Valerie.

Valerie's death remains a substantial and profound influence in Jenn's life. Among the many memories of the experience, one in particular persists. As evening approaches and her son crawls into bed, and in the morning when he wakes up, she feels an unmistakable desire to rub his back. In doing so, she recalls a van-ride conversation with her friend Val on a dusty road in Guatemala. Valerie had made a promise to rub Peter's back when she returned from her trip. Now Jenn fulfills that promise with her own son. Though not as routine as it once was when he was younger, Jenn says it never gets old and is always meaningful.

We didn't find out until after Val died that Julie and Ludovic were engaged to be married. They completed the union the following year and still live in France. They now have three children of their own. Reconnecting with them for this book was wonderful, and I hope someday to visit them and thank them again in person.

I would also like to see Edmundo again. It is my understanding he is doing well and still lives near Santa Elena in north-central Guatemala. I am content to know these reunions will happen at some point in the future.

While meeting with Susan regarding this book, she said, "I don't keep many things. I'm not a pack rat, and if I don't see a use for something, I either recycle it or throw it away. I'm not sure you would find it appropriate, but I saved something for you, if you would like it."

I nodded somewhat cautiously as she left for her office. She soon returned and handed me a small metal cap. The object had internal threads on one side with a concave octagonal shape on the other. It measured approximately an inch and a half in diameter by three-quarter inches in width. In several places, I could see gray casting where the white paint had chipped away. Susan explained the small piece of metal I was holding was part of the sealing and locking mechanism for Valerie's casket.

"I'd completely forgotten I still had it until I saw you today," she said. "For some reason, I kept it." Susan went on to tell me that after we'd selected another casket for the funeral, she had the one Valerie arrived in destroyed. She restated her feelings regarding the metal casket's poor condition, and not wanting it to end up in someone else's hands, she personally took it to a recycling facility and witnessed its destruction herself. Just prior to its crushing, she removed the locking end cap.

The metal cap currently rests on my office desk to the left of my computer screen. I look at its damaged white paint almost every day, a visual symbol of the ill-fated trip.

My feelings of disappointment for not staying to see Valerie placed into the ground struck a chord with Susan. After I told her of my regret, she changed the funeral home's policy regarding burials. She now always asks their clients if they would like to stay and see their loved one's casket lowered into the vault. Though a small number of people request to see this, I am grateful that she allows the ones who do the opportunity to be a part of this final act.

Years went by before I had a gravestone positioned at the cemetery, which was more than curious to many. The grave marker has several symbolic elements, and although it's nothing fancy, it sits in stark contrast to the ones surrounding it. Valerie's grave site is located in one of the oldest parts of the small cemetery, and within twenty-five feet of her plot are headstones with dates ranging from 1851 to 1933. Several of the people commemorated on those stones also died young. To me, this provides a peculiar serene feeling.

Pastor Jeff and I initially saw each other frequently, but he moved on from St. Paul Lutheran and now lives out West. I'm sure he often wondered how I was doing in my spirituality after Valerie's passing. As my family tried to build an alternative life, I questioned a number of previously held truths, including my relationship to the church and God. Pastor Jeff and I have spoken a number of times about Valerie's death and his recollections of the events. One statement is particularly poignant to me.

He said, "I've been through a lot in my many years of service, and Valerie's death was one of the saddest. I had never seen a church community so sad, and to this day it has left a mark on me."

Though many people traveled a considerable distance to attend the funeral service, many others could not make it. On May 12, 2004, a community of friends, relatives, and neighbors came together in a "Celebration of Life" service for Valerie in her hometown of Homedale, Idaho.

Many have honored Valerie in unique ways, such as planting trees, creating a chapel that displayed some of Valerie's favorite photos, attempting to rename a local park, and participating in ongoing American Heart Association fundraising campaigns. Each is a special gift and a great honor to her.

I've discovered that children can be extremely resilient. During the first few weeks after Valerie's death, I tried to read as much as I could about children's ability to process and ultimately deal with the passing of a loved one. The books helped me understand a few basic elements of grief. However, after I read several, they started to sound the same. Susan mentioned a children's grief center called Camp Amanda (now called the Children's Grief Connection) that runs weekend retreats for children who have experienced the loss of a family member. My children attended one of their events in the fall of 2004. The camp was helpful in many ways, though it confirmed the fact that we had a long road ahead of us.

I woefully underestimated the time involved in raising three kids. Cooking; cleaning; laundry; transporting; transporting some more; homework; shopping for supplies, food, and clothes; and making every damn decision about everything all became commonplace and routine. Many of you know this life all too well, but I only now understand its vastness. It is unglamorous and tedious to some and has been many times for me, but I have come to respect this life and am coming to peace with its meaning for me.

Emotions, both positive and negative, filled our years as each member of my family walked a slightly different and circuitous path. The chronicling of these life issues and learning is another topic, but suffice it to say, I had a lot to learn as the only adult staring at three young children who had just lost their mother.

My children have adjusted extremely well and, for the most part, adapted to a life without their mother. They are well-rounded, grounded, and, overall, simply good kids. Of course,

I am so very proud of where their lives have taken them. At their current ages, they have become much more than children.

Valerie's detailed description of her children, their personalities, and what she suspected they would be like when young adults was uncannily accurate. Maybe all moms somehow know, even when their children are very young, what they will be like when they are older. This was insight I did not possess.

The suit coat Peter wore at the funeral, the one that came with the promise that he could burn it after the ceremony, remains intact. It is his decision if, or when, its destruction takes place.

By the end of 2006, the walls of my life seemed to be closing in. I was going down a path that I knew was unsustainable, and something needed to change. I felt overwhelmed and exhausted. I missed Valerie so much it hurt to think about. Cobbled-together birthdays and Christmas presents, spending too much time at work, and worrying about missing the next school event or game put an additional strain on my body.

I understood I was the one placing these burdens on myself and further understood others might have handled the activities and responsibility better than I. Down deep inside, I knew what I needed to do, but that didn't make it any easier. My priorities required an adjustment, so over the first part of 2007, I made plans to quit my job. I spoke with leaders of the company, and some understood and others simply did not. With some semblance of a new plan in place, I walked out the door and ended what I'd known as my career on June 13, 2007.

Financially, I knew this new strategy couldn't last forever. Yet I felt fortunate to have the ability and fortitude to make a substantial change, and I hoped it would enable me to have a greater impact on my children's lives. There was certainly a drive inside me to focus on my family and the children's needs. They had lost their mother—how could I not change my life?

Why I felt this way wasn't completely clear to me for close to four years. It turned out the reason was right in front of me, written on a piece of paper in black and white. All I needed was to read the words Jeff had written in his journal, and additional clarity on the meaning and purpose of my life would come into focus.

*Rod softly spoke to her, telling her that he would take care of the kids.*

I'd forgotten saying those words to Val in the embalming lab of the Guatemalan funeral home and attributed my actions to paternal instincts. I was trying to raise our children in a way I believed she had envisioned. However, upon reading Jeff's journal entry, I realized that the promise to Val had been the impetus to change my life. In discovering this connection, some of the issues I'd been struggling with became clearer, and the awareness brought with it a new level of peace and understanding regarding my life's decisions.

I still love Valerie and have no reason to suspect this will ever change. If there is ever another person in my life, she will need to understand this and not be afraid. She will need to understand, as I do, that love is not finite but infinite.

During the first day and a half of our Central American trip, we took numerous photographs and recorded some video segments. Though I had looked at each photo many times, I didn't watch footage from the video camera for nearly ten years. At first, I simply couldn't, because it would hurt too much. Looking at photographs of Valerie and watching other videos taken during her lifetime were often difficult, yet reassuring as a reminder of the life we had shared—a life full of happiness.

The video taken in Guatemala was different. I understood all too well there would simply never be another photograph, video, or even a single note of her voice I hadn't seen or heard previously. This specific video of Val was yet unknown. There would be images of Valerie I hadn't seen before and words I'd yet to hear. That was enough at times to keep me going. Albeit ever so small, there was still a part of Valerie yet to encounter, and the feeling was mysteriously comforting, knowing I had a discovery yet to make.

Even with years of anticipation, I didn't want to set a specific time or day for its viewing. I knew it would likely be a random moment when an overwhelming urge would hit me, and I would know the time had come to view the tape. The idea of watching the video had once been a daily preoccupation, but over the years, it had moved to the back of my mind. As the ten-year anniversary grew near, once again the thoughts moved to the forefront. On April 4, 2014, as I knelt down by the outside door of our basement to wipe the spring mud off our dog's paws, I eyed the video recorder next to the television. I knew instantly this was the time to watch the video. I could barely contain myself. My daughters were at college, and my son, now a senior in high school, was out with his friends on this Friday night.

I went upstairs just after nine to retrieve the tape out of its special location in the spare bedroom closet. As I passed the hallway, I noticed a half-empty bottle of wine behind the kitchen sink and decided a glass would be appropriate. I placed the tape into the machine and noticed through its clear plastic front that it was nearly to the end.

*Hmm, we must have taken a lot more video than I thought.* I rewound the tape, and my pulse quickened. Somehow, the wine in my glass was already gone, though I couldn't remember drinking it. Nevertheless, the glass was empty, and I had yet to see one scene. Maybe I needed something a little stronger. As the tape continued its high-pitched rewind squeal, I went back upstairs.

I returned and sat on the floor. With my dog to my right and a glass of whiskey to my left, I knew Valerie would appear at any moment on the screen in front of me.

I was a surprised when the first scene was of an eight-year-old boy being goofy in front of the camera. I should have known there would be other people on this particular tape. The sight of my son brought a smile to my face. As he was now six-foot-four, I realized how much the boy on the tape had grown in the past ten years. My daughters made an appearance next. *They are so young,* I thought. There on the screen were small, freckle-faced, carefree kids, innocent and unknowing that in a few short weeks after taking this video, their mother would no longer be alive.

I first heard Valerie's voice in the background, and that made me want to see her face even more. *Why didn't we take more videos of Val?* I asked myself. When she was in the video, she looked beautiful, and to hear her voice again was exceptional.

The tape included a trip to Chicago; a gathering at my cousin's house, where the group sang a song to Valerie for her fortieth birthday; a trip to a local ski hill; and an elementary school concert.

As I watched various scenes flash before me, it showed a glimpse into a former life. My eyes streamed with tears of joy and pride over my family and, at the same time, from a deep sense of loss. The participants appeared to be enjoying their lives—one that no longer existed. A life I now wished I'd enjoyed more.

These initial video snippets acted as an introduction to the main feature film that was about to begin. The first scene opened on Jenn, Jeff and Valerie sitting in the Northwest Airlines lounge about to embark on our trip. They looked a bit tired, perhaps, but overwhelmingly happy and excited. As I suspected, there wasn't a lot of video of our shortened trip, though I was thrilled to see Val was part of many scenes. The recording included segments in San Ignacio, some of the Tikal ruins in the daytime, and then footage of the top of Temple IV at sunset. During the walk back, low light conditions compromised the camera's video quality, though I could still see people's images, and the sound was clear. There was footage of the park ranger with his pistol-grip shotgun slung around his shoulder, Jenn commenting on the incredible amount of fireflies, and Val talking to Jeff and Jenn and laughing about something. The final video clip showed Jenn, Jeff and Val walking away along the path some distance in front of me. Their images then grew darker and darker, and then the video faded to black.

I rewound the tape to the first scene of our trip and watched it again. This time I looked for clues or signs that something might have been wrong with Valerie. I looked closely at the images on the screen. A stumble, shortness of breath, a worried sign on her face—anything could be important. As I'd seen firsthand a decade ago, there was no evidence of a warning sign—at least not one that I could see. That conclusion was fine by me. I appreciated the images for what they were—the last recording of Valerie's life.

It seems I hear Tikal mentioned in the news every so often, and I pay particular attention to any reference to the place. Several books and magazines identify the area as one of the greatest and most mysterious places on earth. I always thought someday, just maybe, I would venture back to the ruins of Tikal with my children. I'm not completely sure I'm ready to return, however. For me it would be a reunion of sorts, a return to a place forever burned into my memory. For my children, its identity has but one singular significance: it is the place where their mother died. Perhaps it would be a reunion for all of us.

From left to right: Jeff, Jenn, Rod, and Valerie

# Acknowledgments

**M**any people came to our aid during this incident and throughout the subsequent years. I am truly thankful for their assistance and commitment to help in any way they could.

Jeff and Jenn, without you I would not have made it. Your selfless acts of kindness, compassion and companionship will live with me always. An ordinary thank you is simply not enough; nevertheless, I will tell you again—thank you. Thanks also for your ongoing friendship. I cherish it greatly.

Ludovic and Julie, your actions were nothing less than heroic, and you went beyond any call of duty. You were willing to do anything you could to save Valerie's life, and your perseverance was exceptional. I thank you for all the efforts made. Within this extraordinary event, you supported me as well. You did not leave my side and continued to sustain my hope for recovery when you likely knew there was little hope. I remain indebted to you for your kindness.

My parents, Mel and Ruby: you took the time repeatedly to do whatever it took to help my family and me. I can never repay you for the assistance you have provided—I love you dearly.

To Valerie's family, relatives and friends: you have continued to embrace my family as your own. Thank you for remaining an essential part of our lives.

I thank my children for trusting me to make the challenging decisions required of a dad. For having the patience to believe that as a family we would indeed make it through difficult times. Perhaps most important is thanks for simply being good kids.

Assistance came from so many other people who helped my family over the years. For everyone who gave in so many ways, from food and memorials to powerful prayers and uncompromising friendship, you have been an immense blessing to us.

I have found, beyond any expectation, that writing a book is very hard work—at least it was for me. To my alpha and beta readers (Nick, Jill, Wendy, Sheila, Stephanie, Bob, Andrea, Joyclyn and Mary), thank you so very much for your comments and necessary criticism. There is no doubt your effort made the book better.

Thanks also to a few exceptional individuals whom I have been fortunate to get to know over the past number of years. You have meaningfully assisted me in seeing my transformed life for what it is and ultimately what would be required to embrace life once again.

# About the Author

Rod Jasmer grew up on one of the 10,000 lakes in Minnesota, near Alexandria. He completed high school and his undergraduate degree in his home state and then ventured west to Idaho to continue his study of geology. It was there he met his future wife, Valerie. In late 1987 they married, he received his graduate degree, and within a few months they packed almost all of their combined possessions into six suitcases and moved to Australia on permanent resident visas. They traveled extensively during their time Down Under, including an extended five-month overland trek throughout Southeast Asia. Upon their return to America, they started a family, and their three children were born over the succeeding five years.

Rod's professional career includes purchasing and starting a number of companies. He has managed the technical direction, personnel advancement and business elements of the firms. He successfully published his first writings in the mid-eighties and has since written hundreds of documents relating to environmental conditions assessment, contaminant analysis and remedial evaluation.

After Valerie's death, it is an understatement to say that his life changed. He eventually quit his professional positions to focus on time with his family. Life with three kids as a single dad wasn't always easy, but they collectively endeavored to maintain a strong family. Travel and adventure continue to be a pastime for Rod, as he finished first in a *Fear Factor Live* competition in Florida and won a 2013 Jeep on *The Price is Right*. After its airing, CBS attached the title of "Jeepologist" to him and the show's promotion.

Rod spends as much time as possible outdoors, doing most any activity the four seasons allow. Skiing, snowmobiling, hiking and snorkeling are some of his favorites. Photography has always been a hobby, with his photographs appearing in newspapers and as part of exhibits, and being auctioned.

Beyond his writing, Rod works as an environmental and business consultant to Union Pacific Railroad and other national clients. He splits his time between living in Linwood, Minnesota, and Park City, Utah.

# Q&A

Over the years, I've been asked various questions about Valerie, the incident, the people who helped, my children, etc. During the writing of this book, editors and beta readers also asked follow-up questions, so I collected the questions and wrote answers to them. A few are included here and many more can be found at RodJasmer.com.

Q: Did Valerie ever mention her fear of the trip the next day or any time during your travels?

A: No. I wish now I would have said something and discussed it. We were happily enjoying the busy trip, and it never came up.

Q: When did you find out that Jenn was initially blaming herself for Valerie's death?

A: Not until years later. I first found out in 2008 when I started to discuss the book with her. However, it wasn't until I conducted another round of interviews with her that she told me how intense her feelings were regarding this subject.

Q: When Val had trouble locating your watch on the nightstand, did you have any thoughts that something might be wrong with her at that time?

A: There was no light in the room, so I didn't think it was that unusual. It was actually somewhat funny when items kept falling off the table and hitting the floor. In retrospect, I've wondered if I might have missed a warning sign.

Q: Do you think that Ludovic and Julie knew from the very beginning that Valerie would not make it?

A: If they did, they did not show it to me. I have not asked them that question.

Q: Were you prepared to have an autopsy completed in Guatemala?

A: I so desperately wanted to find out what had happened to Val that I wouldn't have given it much thought. It was Dr. Carlos who insisted that the autopsy should be performed back in the States.

Q: Were you concerned that your children might find out what had happened to Valerie prior to you telling them?

A: I certainly did not want them to find out, but I didn't think anyone would contact them directly. It would be very different now with the reach of social media.

Q: Did you think to tell Susan that the Guatemalan funeral home would be sending blood along with Valerie?

A: It never crossed my mind. I assumed this was typical of what was done. Susan sent the bottle of blood along with Val's body to the medical examiner, but from my discussions with them, I don't think they even opened or examined the bottle.

Q: Why did you say the purpose of your life became clearer after you read Jeff's journal describing your conversation with Valerie?

A: My life had changed dramatically, and I wasn't sure what I was doing half the time. It was about instincts and just doing what I thought I needed to do. Sometimes it took going down an unhealthy path before I realized I needed to change. Reading Jeff's journal helped me understand many of my actions. It was an affirmation of what I was doing.

# Reading Group Discussions

Chapter 1: Premonition
a) Have you or anyone you know ever had a premonition or an intuition that something would happen? Has this happened to you more than once?
b) What was the intuition? Did it come true?

Chapter 2: Past Experience versus Present-Day Existence
a) Many times it can be easier to talk about doing something than actually following through and doing it. With a busy life, how do you manage this balance?

Chapter 3: The Essentials
a) Some say that preparing for a trip can be as much fun as taking the trip. Do you agree or disagree?
b) What is an essential part of your travel pack?

Chapter 4: Disappearing Sounds

a) Do your loved ones get concerned when you leave on vacation or travel for work?

b) Do you write notes to people before you leave on vacation?

Chapter 5: Back on the Travel Bicycle

a) I discuss some anxiety when arriving at a new destination, particularly a place you have never been previously. Have you ever felt this?

b) Have you ever lost anything or been swindled on vacation?

c) Do you think bottled water is pure no matter where you get it?

Chapter 6: A Great Day

a) How long does it take you to relax and really start to enjoy a vacation: immediately, hours, days, weeks, never?

b) Have you ever accepted a ride from a stranger?

c) Valerie talked about what she thought her children would be like as adults. Have you ever thought about that? Were you accurate in your assessment?

d) Do you prefer photographs of people or landscapes?

e) What is your best travel packing tip?

f) If you have ever been to Tikal, what was your impression and experience?

g) The sudden swarm of fireflies became a metaphor for the book. Have you ever experienced a non-life-threatening event that you knew would dramatically impact your life? What was it?

Chapter 7: The Awakening

a) Do you or your partner ever have nightmares? Are they always a similar dream or do they vary?

b) I describe what I did after realizing that Valerie was in trouble. What would you have done?

Chapter 8: Desperate for Help

a) Have you ever needed to perform CPR on anyone?

b) Have you ever been asked to help someone in need of emergency assistance? What did you do?

c) It is understandable the other people staying in Tikal would have been scared by someone banging on doors and yelling at them from outside their room in the middle of the night. How would you have reacted?

d) Have you ever drawn a conclusion about someone (like Caroline) and then had them prove your original perception was wrong?

e) I have thought about the odds of having three doctors at Tikal on the night we were there. Coincidence or something else?

f) Having someone slap Valerie's face and then strike a forceful blow to her chest was difficult for me to watch. How would you have reacted in this situation?

Chapter 9: It's Already Here

a) When the ambulance arrived near the room, did you wonder where it had come from? Did you immediately question what it might contain in terms of supplies, or were you thinking, like me, this was a real ambulance with all the amenities?

b) Did Ludovic's and Julie's willingness to get into the ambulance and perform mouth-to-mouth CPR surprise you?

Chapter 10: Santa Elena / Flores, Peten

a) Finally reaching the hospital was a relief, but not being able to enter was immediately deflating. Have you ever tried so hard to get somewhere only to be completely disappointed once you got there?

b) Jenn stated that, on any other occasion, she might not have made it over the iron gates, but she was able to do it twice. Has there been a time when you did something without hesitation and now wonder how you did it?

Chapter 11: Planes, Dogs, Military and Money

a) How do you think Jenn felt being in a military facility in the middle of the night without a lot of clothes on and speaking a foreign language?

b) With the focus on saving Val's life, nothing else mattered at that time. It was as though the world had stopped. Has there been a time in your life that everything stopped?

c) I've wondered if we should have asked how many hospitals were in the town and why we were taken to that particular one. Would you have asked these questions?

Chapter 12: Refuting the Unfathomable

a) When do you believe Ludovic and Julie knew Valerie would not make it?

b) Why do you think Ludovic needed to prove to me that Valerie had expired?

c) Have you or anyone you know fainted from hearing or seeing something disturbing?

Chapter 13: Checking the Clock

a) Clearly my thought of taking Valerie out of the hospital and getting back to the States in the same day was an unrealistic plan. Why do you think it seemed like such a real possibility to me?

b)  Have you ever seen a hospital with openings without doors or windows? What could be the purpose?

Chapter 14: The Official

a)  As the day progressed we became more and more frustrated with the hospital staff. My instinct tends to be to isolate myself and figure out a solution alone. This is very different from what Val would have done. How do you react when you need to work through a problem?

b)  What do you think would have happened if the official had smelled alcohol on me or Valerie?

c)  Edmundo's assistance was very helpful and appreciated. Do you think most hotel owners would have provided this level of assistance?

Chapter 15: Waiting to Hear

a)  Jeff remained at Tikal to gather our belongings while Jenn came along in the ambulance. Would it be harder to wait or go in the ambulance? What would you have preferred to do?

b)  At times complete strangers can provide comfort to each other. Have you ever been comforted by a stranger or provided comfort to someone you did not know?

Chapter 16: Weathered Faces and Perplexing Voices

a)  The hospital bathroom was merely a storage closet for new and used medical supplies. Have you ever been somewhere and seen something you would never expect to see at that location?

b)  I thought the men were Catholic priests, but I was speculating. Do you know what ritual they bestowed on Valerie?

Chapter 17: Friend or Foe

a) Even though the other hospital was not a pristine facility, do you think it could have provided additional help for Valerie?

b) It is still a mystery as to why the three local funeral workers showed up at the hospital. What do you think their motivation was?

c) I was not eager to give my passport to anyone. What is your most important possession on a vacation?

Chapter 18: The First Box

a) We never thought to inquire about another part of the hospital until later in the day. Should they have mentioned this to us earlier or was it up to us to inquire about it?

b) The episode with Caesar, the tourism guy, was very strange. Why do you think he came to the hospital?

c) Changing Valerie's clothes was an impactful experience for the three of us. What are your thoughts about this?

d) The old, used, Western-style plywood box casket startled us. Is this something that you would have expected?

Chapter 19: Misery Road

a) Would you have taken the small late-model pickup not knowing that the next vehicle would be an old Suburban?

b) Time moved incredibly slowly during the first part of the trip to Guatemala City. Has there ever been a moment in your life when time virtually stood still?

c) What would be your solution if the third tire had blown without an additional spare?

d) We saw people laughing and received strange looks as we moved slowly through crowded towns. Would this happen in any country?

e) I have wondered many times why I could not transfer Valerie's body when we switched caskets halfway to Guatemala City. What do you think might have been the reason?

f) My mind had some wild thoughts when riding alongside Val's casket in the back of the hearse. Was it lack of food and water, the cramped, dark conditions, or the situation itself that made my mind drift?

## Chapter 20: Guatemala City

a) We thought there might be a possibility that we were in serious trouble and that Fernando would call the police to investigate us. What do you think would have happened if he had made that call?

b) Why do you think Fernando wanted us to conduct the autopsy in Guatemala?

c) After 10:00 p.m. the funeral home was bustling with activity. It seemed everyone was in their best clothing and we looked and felt at our worst. Where have you felt the most out of sync with everyone else?

d) Have you ever hurt yourself and then forgotten about it until later?

e) Suddenly Val's possessions became precious to see and handle. If this has ever happened to you, what were the objects?

## Chapter 21: Poor Connections

a) After a tragedy, whom would you call first?

## Chapter 22: A Promise

a) Would you have expected to find the bloody rags, bag and bottle next to Val at the funeral home? At the time, the material surrounding her did not seem important to me. What would have been your thoughts?

b) It was very important that I tell Val about how I would try and raise our children. If I thought she already knew this, why was it so necessary to say it?

c) Jeff described "seeing death" when Val was on the floor of the bungalow. Do you believe that was what he really saw?

Chapter 23: The Embassy and La Cumbre

a) You can find many ironies in this story. Doesn't it seem ironic that we were spending our nights at a bastion-of-happiness hotel where new families were being formed all around us? Was it serendipitous that Jeff and Jenn had been thinking about adoption? What other examples of irony did you notice?

b) I did not know what to say to other hotel patrons who casually asked me how I was doing. What should I have said?

c) It took a while at the embassy to speak with someone who knew the answers to our questions. Was this a surprise to you?

d) Were you at all surprised when Ms. Sophie and Dr. Carlos told us they were still missing some important documents?

Chapter 24: Not Quite Home

a) Even surrounded by all the people in the airport, I felt completely isolated. Do you think that feeling is common among people? Has it ever happened to you?

b) Have you ever thought that you should have been the one to die instead of your friend or loved one?

c) In many countries, medical treatment that is just minutes away is taken for granted. What else we do frequently take for granted?

Chapter 25: Facing a Formidable Day
a) What is the most difficult thing you have ever had to tell someone?

Chapter 26: Understanding the Meaning of Words
a) It was truly amazing to me the difference between how my adult friends and family reacted to news of Valerie's death versus my children's reactions. Do you think this would be the same for other people? Other situations?
b) There can be certain times when you question what you have done in your life or the accomplishments you've made. This was one of those times for me. Have you ever seriously questioned what you have done in your life?

Chapter 27: Sangria
a) The locking white casket I purchased in Guatemala looked beaten up and stained by the time it reached Susan in America. What do you think happened?

Chapter 28: Inconsequential Selections
a) Even after I told Steve and Eileen that Valerie might not look like herself, they were completely shocked when they saw her. By this time, I was comfortable viewing Valerie's body. Do you think it was the makeup and presentation or just the shock of seeing Valerie not breathing for the first time that made it so hard for others to view Valerie?
b) I couldn't have cared less about most of the funeral arrangements. In your opinion, who is a funeral really for?
c) Telling the story of the incident and talking about Valerie has always been easy for me. Some find it very difficult to talk about loved ones who have passed. What is your comfort zone?

Chapter 29: Driving Away

a) The visitation and funeral felt at times like a series of processions that were unrelated to Valerie. Have you ever been at an event that felt surreal?

b) Many people do not understand the deep remorse I felt leaving Val on top of the ground. Do you know of anyone who has stayed to cover the casket?

c) If you are reading this far, I can hardly believe it, but thank you. As we were leaving the interment, I placed my hand on the top corner of the casket and it suddenly moved on its metal supports. I was shocked and wondered what I had done. I grabbed the casket's side railing hoping it would stop moving in the direction of the large, freshly dug hole. I remembered others touching it before without any movement, but somehow the structure had shifted and it was free to move. Susan was the only other person who saw the movement and quickly came over to help me hold it in place as she directed one of her assistants to secure the latch on the supports. I'm not sure what to think of that. Spiritual message, physics, or something else?

Chapter 30: Understanding the How

a) How important would it be to you to know the specific cause of a sudden death?

Chapter 31: In the Recesses of the Mind

a) Do you believe there could be any connection, on any level, between Jeff's e-mail, Valerie's statement the night before the trip, and the eventual reality of her death?

b) As a scientist, I wanted specific answers, logical sequence, and a conclusion as to why. Few aspects of Valerie's death had those elements. I have tried to change my life to accept this reality and embrace it without wondering why. What are your conclusions?

c)  I have tried to learn what I can from this tragic ordeal. To accept events, people, and moments in life and embrace them for what they are without trying to always figure them out. Has there been an event that changed your perspective on life?

Postscript

a)  If you have children, do (did) you have any bedtime or waking up rituals?

b)  I describe being overwhelmed with the daily routine of raising children. If you have children, how have you managed these tasks?

c)  I waited a long time before watching the video we took on the trip to Tikal. Would you have waited so long?

d)  What do you think of me traveling back to Tikal? Should I bring my children with me?

CPSIA information can be obtained
at www.ICGtesting.com
Printed in the USA
BVOW06*0012020317
477532BV00001B/1/P